SRA THEATRE ARTS

Connections

Level 6

Columbus, OH

The McGraw-Hill Companies

SRAonline.com

 SRA

The **McGraw·Hill** Companies

THEATRE ARTS
Connections

Arts Education for the 21st Century

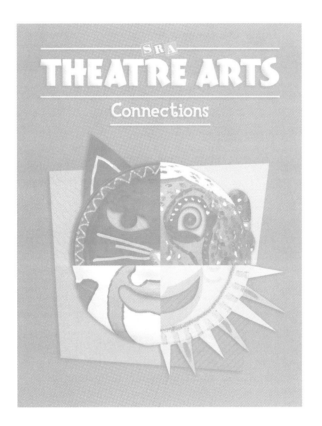

Character Culture Plot Critical Thinking

Creativity Literature Personal Expression

**Theatre Arts education encourages different ways
of learning, knowing and communicating.**

SRA THEATRE ARTS
Connections

All the Resources you need for a Total Theatre Arts Curriculum

Theatre Arts Connections provides everything teachers need to offer meaningful theatre arts education.

Theatre Arts Connections K-6

Thirty-six 15–30 minute Lessons per grade level develop the elements and principles of theatre arts.

Warm-Up activities focus students on lesson concepts.

Step-by-step teacher instructions promote successful lessons.

Creative Expression quick drama activity in every lesson brings concepts to life.

History and Culture featured in every lesson.

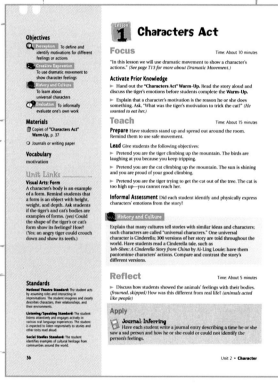

Plus

- **Complete stories and scripts** so teachers have everything they need to be successful

- Unit Openers provide an overview of Unit **concepts and vocabulary** and show theatre's effects across the curriculum.

- Unit Wrap-Up instructions pull unit concepts together as students **create a theatrical production.**

- **Unit Assessments** evaluate understanding.
  - Assessment Rubrics
  - Self-Assessment
  - Quick Quiz

- **Professional Development**

Artsource® Video/DVD

Artsource® Video and DVD offer live performances that apply theatrical elements and principles.

Integrates the four disciplines of art into every lesson

Meet today's standards for theatre arts education

 **Perception**

Develop concepts about self, human relationships, and the environment using drama elements and theatre conventions.

 **Creative Expression**

Create dramatizations and interpret characters, using voice and body. Apply design, directing, and theatre production concepts and skills.

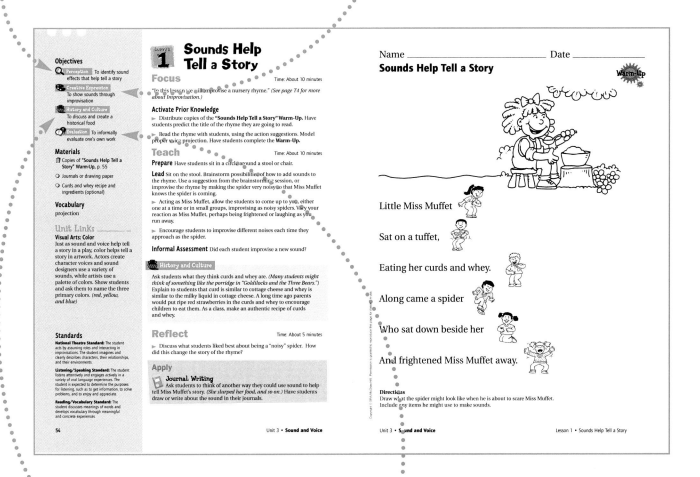

 **History and Culture**

Relate theatre to history, culture, and society.

 **Evaluation**

Respond to and evaluate theatre and theatrical performances.

Theatre Arts and ... Math, Science, Social Studies, Reading and Language Arts

Expand understanding and interest in subject-area studies when students explore theatre arts across the curriculum.

Vocabulary Development Key vocabulary terms are identified and defined to develop the language of theatre.

Reading Themes Make reading themes come to life through dramatic play as students explore a common theme in every unit of *Theatre Arts Connections.*

Theatre's Effects Across the Curriculum Show students how theatre concepts relate to science, math, social studies, reading, and language arts in every unit.

History and Culture Develop historical understanding as students explore theatre history and culture in every lesson.

Literature Integration Actively explore literature with stories and scripts from around the world.

Writing Develop writing skills through Journal activities in each lesson.

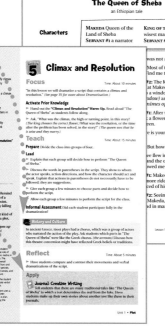

Integrating the Arts

Expose children to music, dance, and visual arts as they explore the theatre arts.

Artsource®
music performances on Video and DVD connect to the elements and principles of theatre.

Visual Arts

Visual Arts connections relate the elements and principles of theatre to the elements and principles of art.

Dance

Artsource®
dance performances on Video and DVD help students connect the elements and principles of theatre to professional dance performances.

Case studies have indicated that students perceive "that the arts facilitate their personal and social development." It also appeared that to gain the full benefit of arts education, students should be exposed to all of the arts, including fine arts, dance, theater, and music.

("Arts Education in Secondary School: Effects and Effectiveness" in Critical Links, p. 76)

Author

Betty Jane Wagner

Betty Jane Wagner is an internationally recognized authority on the educational uses of drama in the classroom and on writing instruction. In 1998, she received the Rewey Belle Inglis Award for Outstanding Woman in English Education from the Women in Literature and Life Assembly of the National Council of Teachers of English. She also received the Judith Kase-Polisini Honorary Research Award for International Drama/Theatre Research from the American Alliance for Theatre and Education.

Recently, she completed a revised edition of *Dorothy Heathcote: Drama as a Learning Medium* (Calendar Islands Publishers, 1999), considered a classic in the field. She wrote *Educational Drama and Language Arts: What Research Shows,* (Heinemann, 1998) and edited *Building Moral Communities Through Educational Drama* (Ablex, 1999).

She co-authored with the late James Moffett three editions of *Student-Centered Language Arts, K–12* (1976, 1983, 1992); and with Mark Larson, *Situations: A Case Book of Virtual Realities for the English Teacher* (1995). She has written several curricula, including *Interaction, Language Roundup,* and *Books at Play,* a drama and literacy program. She has also written numerous chapters in books, such as the *Handbook of Research on Teaching the English Language Arts* and *Perspectives on Talk and Learning,* as well as articles for the National Council of Teachers of English journals.

Wagner is a professor in the Language and Literacy Program of the College of Education at Roosevelt University and director of the Chicago Area Writing Project.

McGraw-Hill: Your Fine-Arts Partner for K–12 Art and Music

McGraw-Hill offers textbook programs to build, support, and extend an enriching fine-arts curriculum from Kindergarten through high school.

**Senior Author
Rosalind Ragans**

Start with Art SRA

SRA/McGraw-Hill presents *Art Connections* for Grades K–6. *Art Connections* builds the foundations of the elements and principles of art across the grade levels as the program integrates art history and culture, aesthetic perception, creative expression in art production, and art criticism into every lesson.

Art Connections also develops strong cross-curricular connections and integrates the arts with literature, *Theatre Arts Connections* lessons, *Artsource*® experiences, and integrated music selections from Macmillan/McGraw-Hill's *Spotlight on Music.*

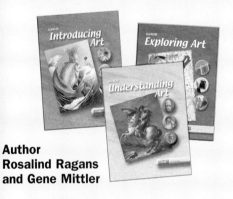

**Author
Rosalind Ragans
and Gene Mittler**

Integrate with Art Glencoe

Glencoe/McGraw-Hill offers comprehensive middle and high school art programs that encourage students to make art a part of their lifelong learning. All Glencoe art programs interweave the elements and principles of art to help students build perceptual skills, promote creative expression, explore historical and cultural heritage, and evaluate artwork.

- Introduce students to the many themes artists express.
- Explore the media, techniques, and processes of art.
- Understand the historical and cultural contexts of art.

**Author
Rosalind Ragans**

ArtTalk offers high school students opportunities to perceive, create, appreciate, and evaluate art as it develops the elements and principles of art.

Motivate with Music Macmillan McGraw-Hill

Macmillan/McGraw-Hill's *Spotlight on Music* offers an exiting and comprehensive exposure to music foundations and appreciation.

Sing with Style Glencoe

Glencoe/McGraw-Hill introduces *Experiencing Choral Music* for Grades 6–12. This multilevel choral music program includes instruction in the basic skills of vocal production and music literacy, and provides expertly recorded music selections in many different styles and from various periods in history.

SRA
THEATRE ARTS
Connections

At every grade level units develop...

- Plot
- Character
- Sound and Voice
- Visual Elements
- Movement
- Subject, Theme, and Mood

Activities

- Theatre Games
- Improvisation
- Pantomime
- Tableau
- Puppetry
- Playwriting
- Reader's Theatre
- Costumes
- Props
- Masks
- Direction

Helps students...

- Understand the **elements** of drama and the **conventions** of theatre.
- Explore **history and culture** through dramatic play.
- Experience literary elements of **plot, setting, and character**.
- Apply design, directing, and **theatre production** skills.
- Develop **critical thinking** and analysis.

Standards

- Meets National and State Standards for Theatre Arts
- Reinforces key subject-area standards in Reading and Language Arts, Listening and Speaking, Social Studies, Science, and Mathematics

Getting Started
The very basics...

Here are some tips for Getting Started with Theatre Arts Connections.

Before School Begins

1. Explore the program components.
2. Plan your year.
   - Consider how often you meet with students. *Theatre Arts Connections* is designed to be a rewarding 15–30 minute weekly activity.
   - Decide how many lessons you can present.
   - Examine your curriculum requirements.
   - Select the lessons that best meet your curriculum requirements.

The First Day of School

1. Give an overview of your goals for theatre arts education.
2. Establish and communicate rules for behavior.

Planning a Lesson

1. Review the lesson in the **Teacher's Edition,** including lesson objectives, in-text questions, and *Creative Expression* activities.
2. Make copies of activities or assessments that will be needed for the lesson.
3. Determine how you will assess the lesson.

"I am enough of an artist to draw freely upon my imagination. Imagination is more important than knowledge. Knowledge is limited. Imagination encircles the world."

-Albert Einstein (1879-1955), physicist

Table of Contents

●◆ Indicates Core Lesson

UNIT 3 Movement

Visual Arts: Rhythm, Movement, and Pattern • Reading Theme: Taking a Stand

UNIT 4 Sound and Voice

Visual Arts: Balance and Emphasis • Reading Theme: Beyond the Notes

UNIT 5 Visual Elements

Visual Arts: Proportion, Distortion, and Scale • Reading Theme: Ecology

UNIT 6 Subject, Theme, and Mood

Visual Arts: Variety, Harmony, and Unity • Reading Theme: A Question of Value

➦ Indicates Core Lesson

Teacher's Handbook

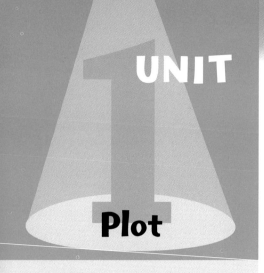

UNIT 1

Plot

Unit Overview

Lesson 1 • **A Plot Is a Chain of Events** The events of a plot make up the action of a play or story. *Theatre Game*

Lesson 2 • **Exposition** Background information is usually revealed in the beginning of a play or story. *Improvisation*

Lesson 3 • **The Major Dramatic Question** The Major Dramatic Question communicates the central conflict of a drama. *Pantomime*

Lesson 4 • **Complications** Series of events can accelerate the conflict in a story or play. *Storytelling*

Lesson 5 • **Climax and Resolution** The climax of a plot is the highest point of suspense; its resolution is the aftermath in which loose ends are usually tied up. *Reader's Theatre*

Lesson 6 • **Unit Activity: Dramatized Literary Selection** This activity will give students the opportunity to act out the elements of plot in a dramatized literary selection.

See pages T3–T20 for more about **Theatre Technique Tips.**

Introduce Unit Concepts

"The plot is the action of a story or play. It contains the events and decisions made by characters that cause the action to move forward."
"La trama es la acción de una historia o drama. Contiene los eventos y decisiones tomadas por los personajes que causan que avance la acción."

Plot

► Ask students how they respond to a television program, book, or movie in which little seems to be happening. *(boredom, disinterest)*

► Tell students that it is not enough to simply have action. The things that happen must have a sequence that makes sense, although this sequence may not always be chronological. That sequence of action is called the plot.

Vocabulary

Discuss the following vocabulary words.

exposition exposición—the time, place, and other background conditions that provide the context for a story or play

Major Dramatic Question Pregunta Dramática Mayor—the key question that a play asks

climax clímax—the point of highest suspense in the plot

resolution resolución o desenlace—the ending of the play or story, in which the problem is usually resolved

Unit Links

Visual Arts: Line, Shape, Form, and Space

► Explain to students that a theatre's stage is empty until it is partially filled with actors, props, and scenery. The playwright and director use this space to focus attention. In the same way, artists use solid forms and empty spaces to make certain parts of their artwork more noticeable.

► Show the image of a painting, such as *Die Erfüllung (The Fulfillment)* by Gustav Klimt. Discuss the shapes and lines. How does the use of space draw attention to certain areas? Have them share personal reactions.

Reading Theme: Perseverance

► Ask students for examples of people who worked hard until they achieved a particular dream or goal. *(Dr. Martin Luther King Jr., and so on)*

► Ask students about some of the areas of their lives in which they are trying to improve or achieve excellence. *(school studies, sports, artistic ability, and so on)* Discuss the benefits of trying to improve one's self.

Teacher Background

Background on Plot

Plot can be defined as a series of events, having a beginning, middle, and an end, that provide the action of a play or story. The plot provides the structure in which the characters live, make decisions, and react to events and to other characters. Some parts of a plot to be studied in this unit include *exposition,* or background details that provide the context of the play or story; *Major Dramatic Question,* which is the most important question the play or story presents and usually answers; *complications,* which are any new elements that change the direction of the action; *climax,* which is the highest point of suspense; and *resolution,* the final part of the play or story.

Background on Playwriting

The playwright is a play's storyteller, and as such, has the fundamental responsibility for providing the plot of the play. It is his or her task to create the structure of events in which the characters act and react.

Research in Theatre Education

"... As we compared the experiences of the children in the respective groups, we saw immediately that the high-arts group consistently outscored the low-arts group on measures of creative thinking and teachers' perceptions of artistic capacities."

—Judith Burton, Robert Horowitz, and Hal Abeles

"Learning Through the Arts: Curriculum Implications."

Differentiated Instruction

Reteach

Have pairs of students choose a favorite story, and ask them to identify its beginning, middle, and end in a few sentences. Discuss their answers.

Challenge

Have students select an event from history that continues to have an impact on contemporary American life. Ask students to identify the historical event as the "cause" and the current condition or situation as one "effect."

Special Needs

Students with disabilities learn best when information engages multiple senses. For example, show students a short clip from an appropriate movie portraying a chain of events; have students identify cause and effect.

Theatre's Effects Across the Curriculum

★ **Reading/Writing**

Reading Response Reading a story and then interpreting its plot through pantomime and improvisation is another way to practice interpreting a written text.

★ **Math**

Prediction When students improvise events in a play or story, they use information from its plot structure to predict events that could take place beyond the play or story's beginning or ending.

★ **Science**

Patterns and Cycles in Nature As students explore the cause-and-effect pattern of plot structure, they can more easily understand cause-and-effect patterns in nature such as animal life cycles, the rock cycle, and the water cycle.

★ **Social Studies**

History Using elements of plot structure to analyze real-life events from history provides students with a way to get an overview of historical events.

★ **Music**

Interpretation Just as students emphasize different elements or emotions when acting, singers can dramatically alter the feeling of a song through interpretation of the phrasing of the lyrics and by the timbre of their voice.

★ **Dance**

Improvisation When students explore a particular idea, event or character through movement improvisation in theatre or dance, they explore personal connections and extend their knowledge.

A Plot Is a Chain of Events

Objectives

 Perception To identify examples of sequence in everyday life and the natural world

 Creative Expression To establish a sequence of events by playing a theatre game

 History and Culture To learn about how folktales often use a sequence of three events to develop a plot

 Evaluation To informally evaluate one's own work

Materials

📄 Copies of "A Plot Is a Chain of Events" Warm-Up, p. 19

⭕ Journals or writing paper

Unit Links

Visual Arts: Line and Shape
Line and shape in art can illustrate a chain of events. Discuss how a work of art sometimes suggests a chain of events that have either led up to or could flow from the scene depicted in the artwork. Remind students that some art forms actually depict a chain of events, as in the frames of a comic strip or a series of tapestries or photographs.

Standards

National Theatre Standard: The student acts by developing basic acting skills to portray characters who interact in improvised and scripted scenes.

Listening/Speaking Standard: The student listens and uses information gained for a variety of purposes, such as gaining information from an interview, following directions, and pursuing a personal interest.

Reading/Comprehension Standard: The student uses the text's structure or progression of ideas such as cause and effect or chronology to locate and recall information.

Focus

Time: About 10 minutes

"In this lesson we will play a theatre game to create a chain of events." *(See page T5 for more about Theatre Games.)*

Activate Prior Knowledge

▶ Hand out the **"A Plot Is a Chain of Events" Warm-Up,** and have students complete it.

▶ Discuss student answers as a class, identifying why information was or was not selected to be part of the chain of events.

Teach

Time: About 15 minutes

Prepare Divide students into groups of four.

Lead

▶ Have each group create a factory assembly line that performs a chain of events to produce a product. Actors can be workers on the assembly line or parts of the machinery. Remind them not to forget to deal with complications when something goes wrong. You may wish to model this with a student volunteer.

▶ After groups have worked on their assembly lines, allow volunteer groups to share their assembly lines with the class. Have the class guess what each end product is.

Informal Assessment Did each student group establish a recognizable chain of events?

History and Culture

Tell students that in many traditional folktales, the structure of a chain of three events is used to communicate the central action of the story. For example, the hero or heroine is given three tasks to accomplish before being granted a wish, or has three encounters with a difficult or dangerous adversary before a goal is achieved. Ask students for examples of tales that use this pattern of events. *(Goldilocks and the Three Bears, and so on)*

Reflect

Time: About 5 minutes

▶ Discuss with students how they decided on the events in the chain that they established.

Apply

📓 Journal: Identifying Cause and Effect

Discuss with students suspenseful chain-of-events examples from movies or television shows. Have students describe how each event in one example leads to the next in their journals.

A Plot Is a Chain of Events

Read the passage below. Then create a chain of events that shows
what Andrew did before he noticed that his list was gone.

Andrew was in trouble. Somewhere, somehow today he had lost the list of things he was supposed to pick up from the store on the way home from school. Normally this would not be such a big deal, but just last night he had a "discussion" with his mother about how he kept losing things. He denied that he did, of course. Now, on the very next day, it would really be embarrassing to admit that it happened AGAIN.

He went over in his mind all the places he had been since he last remembered having the list. He knew he had stuck it in his notebook between his math assignment and his science report. He remembered seeing it at the end of math class. So where had he been since then?

After math he had gone to English and then to history. He stopped by his locker before going to band. From there he went straight to the cafeteria and had lunch. Right now he was in science class. When he got out his report to turn it in, the list was gone. It just was not there. He knew he would have to go back to every place he had been that morning. If he did not find that list, he would never hear the end of it.

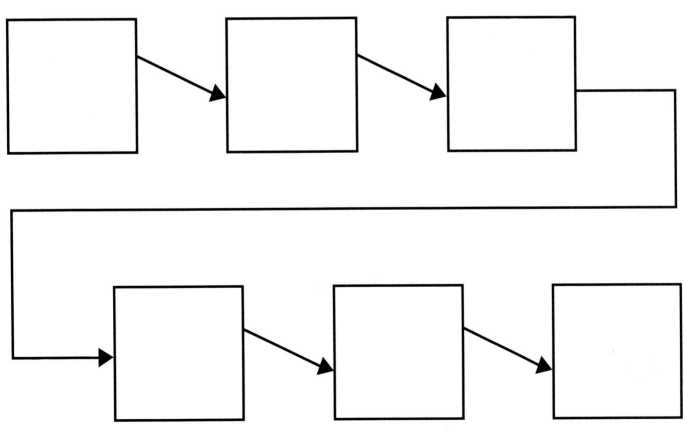

Objectives

Q Perception To use details to identify exposition facts in a situation and consider ways these details can be misleading

Creative Expression To establish exposition facts through the use of improvised movement and words

History and Culture To learn about an exposition exercise used by comedy improvisation groups

? Evaluation To informally evaluate one's own work

Materials

📄 Copies of "Exposition" Warm-Up, p. 21

○ Journals or writing paper

Vocabulary

exposition
improvisation

Standards

National Theatre Standard: The student in an ensemble interacts with invented characters.

Listening/Speaking Standard: The student participates in classroom discussions using effective speaking strategies, for example, asking questions and making observations.

Reading Standard: The student reads regularly in instructional-level materials that are challenging but manageable (text in which no more than approximately 1 in 10 words is difficult for the reader).

Lesson 2 Exposition

Focus

Time: About 10 minutes

"In this lesson we will use improvisation to show details of exposition." *(See page T4 for more about Improvisation.)*

Activate Prior Knowledge

► Hand out the **"Exposition" Warm-Up,** and have students complete it.

► Discuss student answers. Say, "Details such as these at the beginning of a story or drama are called exposition."

Teach

Time: About 15 minutes

Prepare Divide students into three groups.

Lead

► Secretly assign one of the following situations to each group: a spaceship in which students, acting as the crew, show details, such as the ship and their mission; an emergency room in which students, acting as doctors and patients, show details, such as time of day and equipment; and an outdoor concert in which students, acting as performers and audience members, show weather and style of music.

► Allow one minute for preparation, and then have each group improvise its situation for the other groups; have the other groups identify facts of exposition.

Informal Assessment Did each group communicate exposition facts using improvised words and actions?

History and Culture

Tell students that many actors and comedians have trained with improvisational theatre groups; one such group is Second City in Chicago, with which many actors appearing on the television show *Saturday Night Live* once performed. Explain that in comedy improvisation, audience members may choose a situation, such as the situations students were given, and the actors must create further expository details of that situation.

Reflect

Time: About 5 minutes

► Ask students what was most challenging about their improvisations.

Apply

📱 Journal: Personal Writing
Tell students that sometimes exposition is intentionally misleading; a playwright or author may choose to trick an audience or reader. Have students write journal entries explaining the consequences of misinterpreting situations in real life.

Name _____ Date _____

Exposition

Read the passage below. Then use the details in the paragraphs to answer the questions that follow.

Anna awoke with a start and stared into the darkness. Dawn was still some time off, but she knew she could not go back to sleep. She was too scared and too excited, both at the same time. From the street, she could hear the rumble of carts as the farmers made their way to market. Before very long, she would be in a cart herself, along with the rest of her family, on their way to the docks. It was there that their long journey would begin.

She sat up and felt for the candle on the table beside her bed. In another minute, her little room became visible in the golden glow of its light. On the chair by the door was her cloth sack. It held the few things that she would be allowed to take with her.

Anna's mother had already packed the family's clothes. Inside this cloth sack were a few small treasures: some pretty stones, a book with leaves and flowers pressed between its pages, four brightly colored pieces of ribbon, and a necklace with a small silver heart. It was not much to remind her of the place that had always been her home.

She tried to imagine what her new home would be like. Mama had said it was a wild place on the other side of the world far from the king and all their country's troubles. Anna wondered if there would be troubles in her new home. She sighed and decided that she would not think about that right now. She lay back down in her bed and waited for morning to come.

1. What clues show where Anna is?

_____

_____

_____

2. What clues show the time in which Anna lives?

_____

_____

_____

3. What clues show where Anna and her family are going?

_____

_____

_____

Objectives

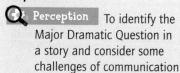 **Perception** To identify the Major Dramatic Question in a story and consider some challenges of communication

Creative Expression To pantomime a plot's Major Dramatic Question

History and Culture To consider how actors pantomimed plots in silent movies

Evaluation To informally evaluate one's own work

Materials
○ Journals or writing paper

Vocabulary
Major Dramatic Question
pantomime

Unit Links _____

Visual Arts: Form
A form can illustrate a plot's central problem. Tell students that artists sometimes create sculptural forms that illustrate the central problem in a historical or fictional story. Ask students how a sculpture illustrating the central problem in "My Dark and Silent World" might look. *(Helen reaching to communicate with Anne wondering how to help, and so on.)*

Standards
National Theatre Standard: The student articulates and supports meanings constructed from his or her and others' dramatic performances.

Listening/Speaking Standard: The student demonstrates nonverbal cues to convey a message to an audience (for example: movement, gestures, facial expressions).

Reading/Comprehension Standard: The student is expected to form and revise questions for investigations, including questions rising from reading, assignments, and units of study.

Lesson 3 — The Major Dramatic Question

Focus
Time: About 10 minutes

"In this lesson we will use pantomime to answer a Major Dramatic Question." *(See page T3 for more about Pantomime.)*

Activate Prior Knowledge
▶ Read aloud **"My Dark and Silent World."**

▶ Ask students what main question might be answered by the rest of this story. *(How would Anne Sullivan change Helen's life?)* Say, "Usually a plot's events answer one central problem. In theatre, this is called the Major Dramatic Question."

Teach
Time: About 15 minutes

Prepare Divide students into groups.

Lead Have students choose a book they recently read as a class. Tell students that each group should decide what the Major Dramatic Question would be if this book were adapted into a play or movie.

▶ After groups have decided, instruct them to choose actions that present the Major Dramatic Question and simultaneously pantomime these actions. Remind them to use safe movement.

▶ If time allows, have volunteer groups share their pantomimes.

Informal Assessment Did each group identify and pantomime the Major Dramatic Question?

History and Culture

Remind students that early movies were silent, so plots were mostly pantomimed. Say, "In the film *Between Showers,* the actor Charlie Chaplin and another man compete to help a woman cross a muddy street. The Major Dramatic Question is 'Will Chaplin win the girl's heart?' How could he work to win her heart?" *(He could push the other man aside.)* How was this film's story influenced by culture?

Reflect
Time: About 5 minutes

▶ Discuss the challenges of using pantomime, and how it helped them understand the plot's meaning.

Apply

Journal: Illustrating
Say, "What challenges do people face when they cannot communicate in their usual way?" *(They have to work harder.)* Challenge students to use pictures to illustrate the Major Dramatic Question of a favorite movie in their journals.

My Dark and Silent World

from *The Story of My Life* by Helen Keller

Helen Keller was little more than a year old when a disease left both her vision and hearing impaired. Helen's life was forever changed when her family hired Anne Sullivan to live with them and work with Helen. She used a teaching method in which she pressed hand signs into Helen's palm. Eventually Helen learned to read and speak, and she later acquired a college education.

This excerpt describes the remarkable ways in which young Helen coped with her world.

I cannot recall what happened during the first months after my illness. I only know that I sat in my mother's lap or clung to her dress as she went about her household duties. My hands felt every object and observed every motion, and in this way I learned to know many things. Soon I felt the need of some communication with others and began to make crude signs. A shake of the head meant "No" and a nod, "Yes," a pull meant "Come" and a push, "Go." Was it bread that I wanted? Then I would imitate the acts of cutting the slices and buttering them. If I wanted my mother to make ice cream for dinner I made the sign for working the freezer and shivered, indicating cold. My mother, moreover, succeeded in making me understand a good deal. I always knew when she wished me to bring her something, and I would run upstairs or anywhere else she indicated. Indeed I owe to her loving wisdom all that was bright and good in my long night.

I understood a good deal of what was going on about me. At five I learned to fold and put away the clean clothes when they were brought in from the laundry, and I distinguished my own from the rest. I knew by the way my mother and aunt dressed when they were going out, and I invariably begged to go with them. I was always sent for when there was company, and when the guests took their leave, I waved my hand to them, I think with a vague remembrance of the meaning of the gesture.

I do not remember when I first realized that I was different from other people, but I knew it before my teacher came to me. I had noticed that my mother and my friends did not use signs as I did when they wanted anything done, but talked with their mouths. Sometimes I stood between two persons who were conversing and touched their lips. I could not understand, and was vexed. I moved my lips and gesticulated frantically without result. This made me so angry at times that I kicked and screamed until I was exhausted.

I think I knew when I was naughty, for I knew that it hurt Ella, my nurse, to kick her, and when my fit of temper was over I had a feeling akin to regret. But I cannot remember any instance in which this feeling prevented me from repeating the naughtiness when I failed to get what I wanted.

The most important day I remember in all my life is the one on which my teacher, Anne Mansfield Sullivan, came to me. It was the third of March, 1887, three months before I was seven years old.

Objectives

 Perception To identify conflict and complications in fictional and real-life stories

 Creative Expression To tell or act out a conflict and further complications

 History and Culture To consider the value of storytelling in many societies and cultures

 Evaluation To informally evaluate one's own work

Materials

📄 Copies of **"Complications" Warm-Up,** p. 25

○ Journals or writing paper

Vocabulary

conflict
complications

Standards

National Theatre Standard: The student analyzes the emotional and social impact of dramatic events in his or her life, in the community and in other cultures.

Listening/Speaking Standard: The student delivers narrative presentations. The student establishes a context, plot, and point of view.

Writing Standard: The student writes for a variety of audiences and purposes and in a variety of forms. The student is expected to write to express, record, develop, reflect on ideas, and to problem solve.

Lesson 4 Complications

Focus

Time: About 10 minutes

"In this lesson we will describe and act out a conflict, adding complications as the story progresses." *(See page T11 for more about Storytelling.)*

Activate Prior Knowledge

▶ Hand out the **"Complications" Warm-Up,** and have students read the story.

▶ Ask, "What caused problems for the spider-woman?" *(the snake)* "What made the problem worse?" *(The snake hid and found her.)*

▶ Tell students that people in a story or play encounter conflict, or events and people that create obstacles for them. Complications, or new twists, make the problem worse.

Teach

Time: About 15 minutes

Prepare Divide students into groups of five or six.

Lead Tell students that each group will create a story about a boy or girl who encounters the conflict of waking up late for school one morning. Three group members will take turns adding complications, such as, "And then she couldn't find her homework," while the remaining group members act them out. The conflict does not have to be resolved. Instruct them to include dialogue.

▶ Have all groups simultaneously tell and act out their stories. If time allows, have volunteers share their stories with the class.

Informal Assessment Did each student add or act out complications?

 History and Culture

Tell students that storytelling is an ancient art form. It has been used to help people in all cultures understand the mysteries of the world. It has been used to reinforce morals and standards of cultures and to teach children. Discuss with students the kinds of stories they have heard as they were growing up. What did they teach them?

Reflect

Time: About 5 minutes

▶ Ask volunteer groups to describe some of their complications. Say, "If this were a play, which complications would add the most excitement?" *(the ones that caused the worst problems)*

Apply

📓 Journal: Narrative Writing

Say, "In 'The Spider Weaver,' the man does not honor the spider-woman's request for privacy." Have students write a story in their journals about complications a character encounters when he or she is trying to have a few moments of privacy.

Name _____ Date _____

Complications

The Spider Weaver

a Japanese folktale

There was once a young farmer who looked up from his work and saw a snake attacking a spider. The man took pity on the spider and chased the snake away. The next morning a beautiful young woman knocked on his door. She was a weaver looking for work. The man could not believe his good luck. He had much cotton, and he needed someone to weave it into cloth he could sell at the market, so he hired the woman.

Before she set to work, she cautioned him that he should never come into the room where she was working. The man thought that it was a strange request, but he agreed. Many days passed in which the woman came every day. The astounding thing was the amount of cloth that she weaved. The man grew more and more curious about the woman. One day, he crept up to the window of the room in which she worked. He could not believe his eyes. Instead of the beautiful young woman, a huge spider sat at the loom eating the cotton, spinning cotton thread out of its body, and then weaving the thread on the loom at an incredible speed. The man realized that the spider he had saved in the field was repaying him and he was grateful. He crept away and said nothing about his discovery.

Soon the man ran out of cotton and had to go to market to buy more. It was a long journey. He started out early in the morning and came home in the late afternoon. Along the way, he stopped to rest. He put the big bundle of cotton that he had bought on the ground beside him and closed his eyes. While the man was asleep, the snake that had attacked the spider came upon the man. The snake hid itself in the large bundle of cotton.

The man awoke and unaware of the snake's presence, took the bundle home and gave it to the woman.

When the woman went into the room, she changed into the spider. Instantly the snake appeared and attacked her. The spider leaped to the window sill in an attempt to escape, but the snake was too fast. Just as the snake was about to gulp the spider down, Old Sun, who had been watching what was happening, reached down and caught hold of the spider with one of his sunbeams. In an instant, the spider was high in the sky and out of danger. In gratitude to Old Sun, the spider used up all the cotton still in its body to decorate the sky with white, fleecy clouds. That is why the word *kumo* is the Japanese word for both *spider* and *cloud*.

Objectives

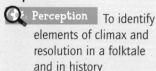 **Perception** To identify elements of climax and resolution in a folktale and in history

 **Creative Expression** To create suspense between the climax and resolution by performing a story as Reader's Theatre

History and Culture To learn about aspects of traditional African drama

Evaluation To informally evaluate one's own work

Materials

📄 Copies of "Climax and Resolution" Warm-Up, p. 27

○ Journals or writing paper

Vocabulary

climax
resolution

Standards

National Theatre Standard: Individually and in groups, the student creates characters, environments, and actions that create tension and suspense.

Listening/Speaking Standard: The student speaks clearly and appropriately to different audiences for different purposes and occasions. The student is expected to present dramatic interpretations of experiences, stories, poems, or plays to communicate.

History Standard: The student understands that historical events influence contemporary events.

Lesson 5 Climax and Resolution

Focus
Time: About 10 minutes

"In this lesson we will perform a story as Reader's Theatre." *(See page T9 for more about Reader's Theatre.)*

Activate Prior Knowledge

▶ Distribute copies of the **"Climax and Resolution" Warm-Up.** Have students read the story.

▶ Say, "What was the moment of highest tension?" *(when the shark revealed that he wanted the monkey's heart)* Tell students that this is called the *climax*; the *resolution* is usually the ending of a story or play, when most loose ends are tied up.

Teach
Time: About 10 minutes

Prepare Divide students into groups of three. Have them sit together.

Lead Say, "Advertisers often place a commercial between the climax and resolution of a television show so viewers will wait for the ending."

▶ Have each group circle the last words spoken in the story before the central problem is resolved, as well as one other exciting moment.

▶ Explain that they are going to read the story as if it were a radio show. Each group should assign the roles of monkey, shark, and narrator. After each circled line, they should create a short commercial break for an imaginary product. For example, they could say, "And now, for a word from our sponsor Snick-Snacks, the best pretzels in the world."

▶ Allow time for planning, and have volunteers perform.

Informal Assessment Did each pair correctly identify the climax and perform the story as Reader's Theatre?

History and Culture

Tell students that many African traditions of drama combine songs, pantomimes, dances, and storytelling. Added effects include costumes, masks, and drumming. Ask students what feeling rhythmic drumbeats could create during a story's climax. *(suspense, excitement)*

Reflect
Time: About 10 minutes

▶ Discuss with students how they built suspense in their radio dramas.

Apply

Journal: Inferring
Have students identify a historical event they have been studying, identify a problem associated with it and how it was resolved, and explain any present day effects of this event in their journals.

Climax and Resolution

A Monkey's Heart

an East African folktale from *The Lilac Fairy Book* by Andrew Lang (Adapted)

A long time ago a large tree hung over the deep sea below a cliff. The tree was full of fruit, and every day at sunrise a big gray monkey sat in the branches. One day the monkey noticed a shark watching her from below with greedy eyes.

"Can I do anything for you, my friend?" asked the monkey politely.

"Oh! If you only would throw me down some of that fruit," answered the shark. "I am so very, very tired of the taste of salty fish."

"Well, I don't like salt myself," said the monkey, "so if you will open your mouth I will throw this juicy *kuyu* into it," and, as she spoke, she pulled one off a branch and dropped it in the shark's mouth.

"Ah, how good!" cried the shark. "Send me another, please."

For weeks the monkey and the shark ate together. One day the shark said, "You have been so kind. Why don't you come visit my home?"

"I should like nothing better," cried the monkey. "But how could I get there?"

"You have only to sit on my back," replied the shark, "and not a drop of water shall touch you." So the next morning the shark swam close up under the tree and the monkey dropped on his back.

The sun had risen and set six times when the shark suddenly said, "My friend, I must tell you something."

"What is it?" asked the monkey. "Nothing unpleasant, I hope?"

"Oh, no! It is only that the king of my country is very ill. The only thing to cure him is a monkey's heart."

"Poor thing," replied the monkey, thinking quickly how she might trick the shark. "But you should have told me this before. I would have brought my heart with me."

"Your heart! Why isn't your heart here?" said the shark.

"Oh, when monkeys leave home we always hang up our hearts on trees. However, perhaps you won't believe that, so let us go on to your country as fast as we can."

The shark believed her. "But there is no use going on if your heart is not with you," he said at last. "We had better turn back to the town, and then you can fetch it."

Of course, this was just what the monkey wanted, but she was careful not to seem too pleased. In three days they caught sight of the *kuyu* tree hanging over the water. With a sigh of relief the monkey caught hold of the nearest branch and swung herself up.

"Have you got it?" asked the shark.

"My dear friend," answered the monkey with a chuckle, "do you take me for a silly donkey? I hope when you go home you will find the king better. Farewell!" And the monkey disappeared among the green branches, and was gone.

Objectives

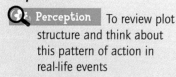 **Perception** To review plot structure and think about this pattern of action in real-life events

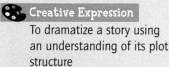 **Creative Expression** To dramatize a story using an understanding of its plot structure

History and Culture To apply research about life aboard a nineteenth-century New England fishing vessel to the events in the story

Evaluation To thoughtfully and honestly evaluate own participation using the four steps of criticism

Materials

- Copies of "Harvey's First Catch," pp. 124–126
- Copies of the **Unit 1 Self-Criticism Questions**, p. 32
- Copies of the **Unit 1 Quick Quiz**, p. 33
- *Artsource*® Performing Arts Resource Package (optional)

Standards

National Theatre Standard: The student researches by using cultural and historical information to support improvised and scripted scenes.

Lesson 6

Unit Activity: Dramatized Literary Selection

Focus

Time: About 10 minutes

Review Unit Concepts

"Plot is the chain of events that create the action in a story or play. The central problem or Major Dramatic Question drives a play's action. Exposition provides information about the time, place, and general circumstances of a play or story. A series of complications changes the direction of the action. The climax is the highest point of suspense; it answers the Major Dramatic Question. The resolution is the aftermath of the action." "La trama es la cadena de eventos que crean la acción de una historia o drama. El problema central o Pregunta Dramática Mayor dirige la acción de un drama. La exposición da información sobre el tiempo, el lugar y las circunstancias generales de una historia o drama. Una serie de complicaciones cambian la dirección de la acción. El clímax es el punto máximo de suspenso; contesta la Pregunta Mayor Dramática. La resolución o desenlace es el periodo posterior de la acción."

▶ Review with students the ways in which they explored the different parts of the plot structure.

▶ Review the unit vocabulary on page 16.

History and Culture

Explain to students that many of the unfamiliar words in the story refer to fishing boats of the nineteenth century and to fishing in general. Have some students research these words' meanings. Provide a chart or bulletin board for students to post meanings of words as they find them. Have another group investigate the life of New England fishermen in the nineteenth century using the Internet or books. Give students time to share their findings with the class. Have each student write a paragraph about a day aboard a nineteenth-century fishing boat, using three researched words.

Classroom Management Tips

The following are tips for managing your classroom during the **Rehearsals** and **Activity**:

✔ **Set Ground Rules** Tell students that whenever you say "freeze" during this activity, they must stop whatever they are doing and stay in the same position they were in when you said it. Explain that if they cannot participate appropriately, they will have to sit at their desks. Seeing the other students having fun may help them choose to follow the ground rules next time.

✔ **Encourage Creativity** During the **First Rehearsal**, compliment students who come up with original questions or responses.

✔ **Take the First Risk** When you take on the role of Harvey, model for students the confusion and spoiled attitude the character should exhibit.

Teach

First Rehearsal

▶ Distribute copies of **"Harvey's First Catch"** on pages 124–126. Have students follow along with you as you read the story aloud. Tell students to circle any unfamiliar words and discuss them (see **History and Culture**).

▶ Say, "We will improvise Harvey's rescue from the ocean—an event that occurred before the events in "Harvey's First Catch." Have volunteers assume the roles of the captain and Dan; all other students will portray crew members. Tell them that you will take the role of Harvey. The action will pick up right after Harvey has been pulled out of the ocean and rescued. The captain, Dan, and the crew members want to know who Harvey is and where he came from. Harvey explains, but they do not believe him. *(See page T6 for more about Dramatization.)*

▶ After a few minutes say "freeze." Have a volunteer become Harvey and invite different volunteers to become the captain and Dan. Repeat the dramatization.

Second Rehearsal

▶ Have students identify the central problem, complications, climax, and resolution of "Harvey's First Catch."

▶ Have the class count off by threes, and have each group assign the roles of the captain, Dan, and Harvey for a dramatization of the excerpt's significant events. Allow groups to dramatize simultaneously.

Plot Activity

▶ Have students alter the room appropriately to create space for the activity. Tell students that they are going to act out "Harvey's First Catch." Explain that you will act as narrator. They will do the dramatization in two parts:

Part One: They will begin with the scene in which Harvey catches his first fish. Ask for volunteers who have not yet done so to play Harvey, Dan, and the captain. The other students will be crew members.

Part Two: They will go beyond the story's ending, showing what happens after Dan and Harvey get back on the fishing boat with Harvey's halibut.

▶ Have students improvise each part. Tell them to freeze when you think it is time to stop. Have students develop criteria for evaluation of the plot activity, and use it to discuss the dramatization.

Standards

National Theatre Standard: The student acts by developing basic acting skills to portray characters who interact in improvised and scripted scenes. The student analyzes descriptions, dialogue, and actions to discover, articulate, and justify character motivation, and the student invents character behaviors based on the observation of interactions, ethical choices, and emotional responses of people.

Unit Links

Visual Arts: Line, Shape, Form, and Space

Viewing art containing elements such as line, shape, form, and space can be contrasted with viewing a performance. Tell students to think about differences between an art viewer and a play's audience member. The viewer of the artwork is simply viewing a finished work. However, the audience member can affect a dramatic performance by giving immediate feedback and continuous interaction. Discuss with students different interactions an audience can have with a dramatized plot. *(laughter, applause, silence)* Have students guess the effect of these reactions on the performers.

Theatrical Arts Connection

Television Show or describe the part of the plot of a television program that demonstrates the difference between the climax and the resolution. Discuss what the resolution scene contributes to the story. Point out to students that some programs, such as soap operas, have little or no resolution. Discuss the effects this has on the audience.

Film/Video Have students view the opening scene of a movie with which they are not familiar, such as a 1940s film noir movie. Stop the viewing before the action of the plot actually begins. Discuss the exposition facts that they were able to discern, and have students predict the plot development.

Standards

National Theatre Standard: The student uses articulated criteria to describe, analyze, and constructively evaluate the perceived effectiveness of artistic choices found in dramatic performances.

Reflect

Time: About 10 minutes

Assessment

▶ Have students evaluate their participation by completing the **Unit 1 Self-Criticism Questions** on page 32.

▶ Use the assessment rubric to evaluate the students' participation in the **Unit Activity** and to assess their understanding of plot.

▶ Have students complete the **Unit 1 Quick Quiz** on page 33.

	3 Points	2 Points	1 Point
Perception	Gives full attention to review of unit concepts and vocabulary words. Masters an understanding of problems and complications in real life.	Gives partial attention to review of unit concepts and vocabulary words. Is developing an understanding of problems and complications in real life.	Gives little attention to review of unit concepts and vocabulary words. Has a minimal understanding of problems and complications in real life.
Creative Expression	Exhibits a clear understanding of the plot structure of the story as evidenced in the words and actions of the character(s) portrayed and contributes to class discussions.	Exhibits some understanding of the plot structure of the story as evidenced in the words and actions of the character(s) portrayed and contributes to class discussions.	Exhibits a minimal understanding of the plot structure of the story as evidenced in the words and actions of the character(s) portrayed and only somewhat contributes to class discussions.
History and Culture	Writes a paragraph about a day aboard a nineteenth-century fishing boat using three of the researched vocabulary words.	Writes a paragraph about a day aboard a nineteenth-century fishing boat using two of the researched vocabulary words.	Writes a paragraph about a day aboard a nineteenth-century fishing boat using one of the researched vocabulary words.
Evaluation	Thoughtfully and honestly evaluates own participation using the four steps of art criticism.	Attempts to evaluate own participation, but shows an incomplete understanding of evaluation criteria.	Makes a minimal attempt to evaluate own participation.

Apply

▶ Ask students, "Do people in real life experience parts of a plot, such as a problem or complications, in their everyday lives?" *(yes; sometimes)*

▶ Ask them to think of a time recently when they learned to do something for the first time or were in an unfamiliar situation. How did they feel at the beginning of this experience? While they were learning or adjusting? Afterward? What problems and complications did they experience?

View a Performance

Plot in Musical Storytelling

► Have students identify elements of appropriate audience behavior when listening to an audio performance, including respectful silence and attention. Have them agree to apply this behavior during the performance.

► If you have the **Artsource®** audiocassette or DVD, have students listen to the excerpts from "The Boy Who Wanted to Talk to Whales," a folktale retold by the Robert Minden Ensemble, which uses conventional instruments, found objects, such as cans and saws, and acoustic inventions, such as the Waterphone.

► Have students discuss and write answers to the following questions:

Describe What events happen in the boy's dream? *(He finds himself in a boat and has trouble keeping the boat afloat because of a huge storm.)*

Analyze What is the Major Dramatic Question of the dream section? *(Will the boy survive the storm?)* How do you think the sections about the tree growing over the mountains and the whales listening to the music fit into the sequence of the story? *(Answers will vary.)* How do the music and the narrator's voice help tell the story? *(The beginning music creates a dreamy feeling that turns into the sounds of a storm; the sound of the narrator's voice changes to reflect the conflict, and so on.)*

Interpret Compare and contrast the feeling of movement created by the music with movement in dance.

Decide What do you think happens next in his dream? How do you think he eventually communicates with the whales?

"The heart of improvisation is transformation."

—Viola Spolin (1906-1994), director/actress

LEARN ABOUT
CAREERS IN THEATRE

Say to students, "How does a scenic designer contribute to the plot of a play?" *(He or she provides the environment where the action takes place. The designer may also include certain items in the environment that provide the audience with exposition facts.)* Explain to students that the designer's job is to shape and fill the stage space, and to make the world of the play visible and interesting to the audience. The designer must work with the director and take into account actors' needs. Sometimes the set will have many realistic details; other times, a set may be intentionally sparse. Ask students to imagine they are scene designers, and have student groups draw a set or build a model for a drama of "Harvey's First Catch." You may wish to ask interested students to investigate the training that is necessary to become a scene designer and report their findings to the class.

Standards

National Theatre Standard: The student analyzes the emotional and social impact of dramatic events in his or her life, in the community, and in other cultures. The student explains the knowledge, skills, and discipline needed to pursue careers and vocational opportunities in theatre, film, television, and electronic media.

Name _____ Date _____

Unit 1 Self-Criticism Questions

Think about how you contributed to the action of the plot in the dramatization of "Harvey's First Catch." Then answer the questions below.

1. **Describe** What things did you say and do as a character in the dramatization that contributed to the forward action of the plot?

   _____

   _____

   _____

2. **Analyze** How did your words and behavior provide complications or lead to the climax and resolution of the dramatization?

   _____

   _____

   _____

3. **Interpret** How are you like and unlike your character? Was it an easy or hard part to play? Why?

   _____

   _____

   _____

4. **Decide** If you could do this activity again, would you change anything you did? Why or why not?

   _____

   _____

   _____

Name _____ Date _____

Unit I Quick Quiz

Completely fill in the bubble of the best answer for each question below.

1. Plot is
- Ⓐ the main character in a story or play.
- Ⓑ the main idea of a story or play.
- Ⓒ the audience's response to a story or play.
- Ⓓ the sequence of events in a story or play.

2. The plot's complications are
- Ⓕ the events that change the course of action of the story or play.
- Ⓖ the research that is necessary to write a story or play.
- Ⓗ the personality of the main character in a story or play.
- Ⓙ the very last event that takes place in a story or play.

3. Every plot has
- Ⓐ a chain of events.
- Ⓑ a beginning, a middle, and an end.
- Ⓒ a climax.
- Ⓓ all of the above.

4. Which sentence is true?
- Ⓕ The plot of a story or play must be short.
- Ⓖ Conflict and complications provide excitement in a play or story.
- Ⓗ Actors do not have to pay any attention to the plot of a play or story.
- Ⓙ The time and place of a play are never important to its plot.

5. Major Dramatic Question is defined as
- Ⓐ "the key character in a play."
- Ⓑ "the most exciting part of a plot."
- Ⓒ "the key question a play asks."
- Ⓓ "the background information of a story or play."

6. During the exposition of a plot,
- Ⓕ there is no sequence of events.
- Ⓖ new events complicate the plot's problem.
- Ⓗ the problem of a plot is solved.
- Ⓙ characters and background information are introduced.

Score _____ (Top Score 6)

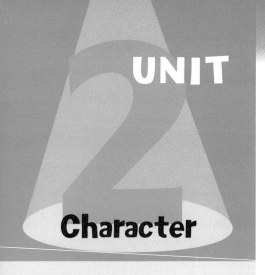

UNIT 2

Character

Unit Overview

Lesson 1 • Character Motivations A character's speech, feelings, and action are a result of his or her motivations. *Sensory Recall*

Lesson 2 • Protagonists and Antagonists As the main character, the protagonist has a goal to be achieved; an antagonist creates obstacles to the achievement of that goal. *Improvisation*

Lesson 3 • Internal Characterization Actors use internal characterization methods, such as emotional recall, to help them experience a character's inner life. *Emotional Recall*

Lesson 4 • External Characterization Actors use external characterization methods to help them move and appear as a character. *Pantomime*

Lesson 5 • Characters Solve a Problem Characters in a drama often work together to solve the central problem. *Improvisation*

Lesson 6 • Unit Activity: Scripted Monologue This activity will give students the opportunity to write and perform a monologue.

See pages T3–T20 for more about **Theatre Technique Tips.**

Introduce Unit Concepts

"Characters are the people, and occasionally personified animals or objects, in a drama or story." **"Los personajes son las personas, y ocasionalmente animales personificados u objetos, en drama o historia."**

Character

▶ Discuss with students different types of characters they have encountered in books, television programs, video games, and films. Remind them that animals and inanimate objects are sometimes personified, or given human characteristics, and become characters.

▶ Identify ways an actor can communicate information about a character, such as age or personality. *(voice, body, and so on)*

Vocabulary

Discuss the following vocabulary words.

character personaje—a person or animal in a play or story

protagonist protagonista—the main character in a plot who is trying to achieve a goal

antagonist antagonista—a character in a plot who puts obstacles in the protagonist's way

Unit Links

Visual Arts: Color and Texture
▶ Explain to students that just as an actor in formal or informal theatre uses words and body language to communicate a character's ideas and feelings, an artist uses color to communicate ideas and feelings in artwork. Discuss what colors students associate with excitement, anger, and sadness. *(yellow, red, blue, and so on)*

▶ Show students an image of a painting with color and texture, such as *Young Spanish Woman with a Guitar* by Pierre Renoir. Ask students to suggest the feeling these colors evoke. *(The warm reds and yellows create a happy and excited feeling, and so on.)* Have students move as the character from the painting, demonstrating this emotion.

Reading Theme: Ancient Civilizations
▶ Ask students to respond to the following statement: "Those who refuse to learn from the mistakes of the past are destined to repeat them." Discuss how this statement might apply to a person's life. *(A person who never gets up on time will always have to rush.)*

▶ Have students suggest some ancient civilizations. *(Rome, Greece, Egypt, the Incans and Aztecs)* What could we learn by studying the history of these civilizations? *(the problems with war, and so on)*

Teacher Background

Background on Character

Characters can be defined as the people, and sometimes personified objects or animals, that execute the action of the plot of a play or story. A character's motivations in a play flow from his or her objectives. The protagonist is the character who has a goal to be achieved. The antagonist is the character who provides obstacles that stand in the way of realizing the goal.

Background on Acting

Much of this unit is devoted to techniques actors use to build a character. In internal characterization, the actor recreates in himself or herself sensations, feelings, and experiences that apply to character portrayal. In external characterization, the actor explores a character from the outside in, working to perfect physical traits that show a character's inner life. Many actors combine these techniques.

Research in Theatre Education

". . . when children have been involved in the process of integrating creative drama with reading they are not only able to better comprehend what they've read and acted out, but they are also better able to comprehend what they have read but do not act out, such as the written scenarios they encounter on standardized tests."

—Sherry DuPont

"The Effectiveness of Creative Drama as an Instructional Strategy to Enhance the Reading Comprehension Skills of Fifth-Grade Remedial Readers"

Differentiated Instruction

Reteach
Have students choose a favorite movie or television character and categorize details under headings such as *physical appearance, clothing, voice, what the character says about him or herself,* and so on.

Challenge
Have students explore an interactive Web site, such as *Odyssey in Egypt* (**www.website1.com/odyssey/ week1/home.html**). Have students write a monologue of an archaeologist describing his or her work.

Special Needs
To reinforce concepts of external characterizations in this unit, have students identify someone that they admire and describe (or imitate) the way that this character walks, stands, and talks.

Theatre's Effects Across the Curriculum

★ **Reading/Writing**
Reading Response Reading a story and then analyzing descriptive details about its characters through dramatic movement is another way to practice interpreting a written text.

★ **Math**
Problem Solving When students become characters faced with a problem during an improvisation, they learn more about all the characters as they interrelate to solve the problem.

★ **Science**
Collecting Data Students collect information useful in portraying characters by sensory and emotional recall as well as by observation.

★ **Social Studies**
History Using improvisation to portray characters from a specific period of history gives students a better understanding of everyday life of that time.

★ **Music**
History and Time As students identify with historical characters' dilemmas and choices, they can apply that understanding to musical theatre, in which character dilemmas and choices are often revealed through song.

★ **Dance**
Sensory Recall Theatre skills sharpen sensory awareness, making students more confident and able to interpret past sensory experiences through dance.

Objectives

 Perception To understand that a character's motivations flow out of that character's objective

 Creative Expression To use sensory recall to express a range of sensations useful in portraying characters

 History and Culture To learn about the connection between Egyptian drama and hieroglyphics

Evaluation To informally evaluate one's own work

Materials

○ Journals or writing paper

Vocabulary

objective
motivation
sensory recall

Standards

National Theatre Standard: The student demonstrates acting skills (such as sensory recall, concentration, breath control, diction, body alignment, control of isolated body parts) to develop characterizations that suggest artistic choices.

Listening/Speaking Standard: The student listens actively and purposefully in a variety of settings.

Reading/Comprehension Standard: The student analyzes characters, including their traits, motivations, conflicts, points of view, relationships, and changes they undergo.

 Lesson 1 # Character Motivations

Focus
Time: About 10 minutes

"In this lesson we will use sensory recall to better understand and act as a character." *(See page T15 for more about Sensory Recall.)*

Activate Prior Knowledge

▶ Read aloud **"Kiya."** Have students listen for sensory details.

▶ Explain that a character's objective is his or her goal; this objective creates a character's motivations, or reasons for speech and action. Discuss the objective that motivated Kiya to go to the market in the heat. *(She wanted to get ready for her cousin's visit.)*

Teach
Time: About 15 minutes

Prepare Divide students into groups of four.

Lead

▶ Have students close their eyes and remember a sporting event. Ask questions related to the physical details of the event, such as "What did you smell? Were you hot or cold?" Discuss details they recalled.

▶ Have each group choose one of the following: baseball players on the bench, coaches, fans, or workers selling refreshments. Students should use one sensory detail to help them identify with their characters. Each character should have an objective that motivates his or her behavior. Remind students to safely use their voices and bodies. Have all students improvise a short scene as these characters.

Informal Assessment Did each student attempt to use sensory recall and participate in the improvisation?

 History and Culture

Explain that ancient Egyptian ritual drama is one of the oldest known dramatic forms. Some scholars believe certain hieroglyphics represent ancient dramas performed by priests. If possible, show examples of hieroglyphics. Discuss possible motivations the priests had to perform these dramas, such as celebration.

Reflect
Time: About 5 minutes

▶ Have students clearly describe their characters' objectives, their relationships, and the details of their surroundings.

Apply

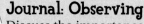 ### Journal: Observing
Discuss the importance of observation in science and theatre. Have students write journal entries listing actions observable at a baseball game and possible motivations for the actions.

Kiya

Kiya had been at the market, and now, after a long walk in hot afternoon sun, she was almost home. It was a typical summer day in ancient Egypt. The sun beat down unmercifully, baking the road, the stones—everything, including her. The long walk seemed longer than usual today and had left her feeling sticky and uncomfortable. She would never normally have gone to the market at such a hot time of day.

With a sigh of relief, she stepped through the doorway of the house where she lived. As she moved from the shadowy anteroom into the kitchen, the cooler air felt wonderful. She went straight to an urn on a shelf and poured herself a cup of water. Its wet, clean taste was welcome relief to the dry, parched feeling in her mouth.

Now that she was out of the heat, she began to feel excited once more. Inarus was coming! She set out the ingredients for tonight's dinner, which she had bought at the market, beside the golden-brown barley and wheat cakes that her mother had prepared early that morning. Beside them, a jug of honey stood ready to be spread on the wheat cakes. Kiya could already taste its sweetness. Also on the table was a bowl of figs. They looked plump and ripe. She picked up the bowl and inhaled the flowery scent of the fruit. She was getting hungry.

From another room in the house came the scraping sounds of furniture being moved. Her mother was determined to have everything ready for their cousin Inarus who was arriving tonight. She usually did not clean in the heat of the afternoon.

As she began to prepare the table for the special meal, she smiled in anticipation of Inarus's visit. Soon his laughter would fill the rooms of their house. He would tease her, of course, but that was all right. In addition to being cousins, they were also good friends.

Objectives

 Perception To understand the terms *protagonist* and *antagonist*

 Creative Expression To use improvisation to explore characters who are protagonists and antagonists

 History and Culture To consider different kinds of protagonists portrayed in plays, film, and television

Evaluation To informally evaluate one's own work

Materials

📄 Copies of **"Protagonists and Antagonists"** Warm-Up, p. 39

○ Journals or writing paper

Vocabulary

protagonist
antagonist

Standards

National Theatre Standard: The student acts by developing basic acting skills to portray characters who interact in improvised and scripted scenes.

Listening/Speaking Standard: The student asks questions and makes comments and observations that reflect understanding and application of content, processes, and experiences. The student participates in classroom discussions using effective speaking strategies (for example, asking questions, making observations).

Writing Standard: The student writes for a variety of audiences and purposes, and in a variety of forms.

 Lesson 2

Protagonists and Antagonists

Focus

Time: About 10 minutes

"In this lesson we will use improvisation to explore protagonists and antagonists." *(See page T4 for more about Improvisation.)*

Activate Prior Knowledge

▶ Hand out the **"Protagonists and Antagonists" Warm-Up.** Have students read the story.

▶ Ask, "Name the protagonist and antagonist. What is the protagonist's objective? How does the antagonist make it hard for Marius to achieve his goal?" *(Marius—he wants to apprentice; Lucius—he doesn't want to)*

Teach

Time: About 15 minutes

Prepare Divide students into pairs. Have them clear an area.

Lead

▶ Tell them they are going to improvise a conversation between Marius and Lucius after the shop closed that day.

▶ Tell students that when you say, "Freeze," the first improvisation will stop, and each pair of partners will switch roles. When you say, "Begin again," they will repeat the improvisation in their new roles.

Informal Assessment Did each student act as both the protagonist and the antagonist?

 History and Culture

Tell students that in some plays, films, and television programs, the protagonist is a hero or heroine who "saves the day" while seeming perfect. However, in other productions, the protagonist has weaknesses. This type of protagonist often seems more believable and appealing. Ask students if this type of protagonist would be more challenging for an actor to portray. *(yes, because it's more realistic)*

Reflect

Time: About 5 minutes

▶ Ask, "How did each character's objective relate to what he said and did?" Discuss the oral, aural, visual, and kinetic aspects of the improvisation.

Apply

📱 Journal: Switching Viewpoints

Say, "Point of view affects the roles of characters. For example, if Lucius told this story, who would be his antagonist?" *(his father)* Have students choose a movie or book, and write a journal entry from its antagonist's point of view.

Protagonists and Antagonists

Read the story below. This story is set in ancient Greece. The **protagonist,** or main character, has a goal he or she is trying to achieve. The **antagonist** makes it difficult for the protagonist to achieve this goal.

Marius sighed as he looked around the workshop. He had worked until dark yesterday to be sure that everything was in order. The floor was swept, and all the pieces of wood of various sizes were neatly stacked against the walls. The workbenches were wiped clean of sawdust and wood shavings. All the tools had been oiled and were laid out neatly in readiness for the day's work. Marius was satisfied with his accomplishments, but he knew that by the end of the day, all that work would have to be done again. The woodworking shop was a beehive of activity every day, and there was no time for clean-up until after the shop closed in the late afternoon.

The problem was that Marius would not be able to get it ready for the next day's work. It was his brother Lucius's turn tonight, and Lucius would do a terrible job. Uncle Julian, who owned the shop, had agreed to take Marius and Lucius on as apprentices to learn the trade. Marius was thrilled. He loved the smell of the wood and the beautiful and practical things that were made from it. He wanted to learn how to make those things more than anything in the world. Lucius,

however, hated the idea of working in the shop. He wanted to become a solider in the Roman legions, to go away and have adventures. Their father had other ideas and had convinced his brother Julian to take them both on as a special favor.

Marius knew Uncle Julian was not pleased. Father was determined that both boys apprentice in the same place, and Marius was afraid Uncle Julian would send them both home. If that happened, his dream of learning this trade would be gone.

When they had begun work three weeks ago, Uncle Julian had explained their tasks. At the end of the first week, Lucius was already making excuses. He did not feel well. It got dark before he could finish. He could not remember the tasks. All the excuses added up to the same thing: he was not doing his share of the work, and the work he *was* doing was inferior. Things would not go on this way much longer.

Marius thought about what he could do. He knew he had better begin by talking to Lucius, and he had better do it before it was too late.

Objectives

Perception To identify situations in which actors might need to use emotional recall

Creative Expression To use emotional recall to recreate a past emotion

History and Culture To connect emotional recall with Stanislavsky's acting theory

Evaluation To informally evaluate one's own work

Materials

📄 Copies of "Internal Characterization" Warm-Up, p. 41

⭕ Journals or writing paper

Vocabulary

emotional recall
Method acting

Unit Links

Visual Arts: Texture

A remembered texture can evoke remembered emotions. Tell students to choose one tactile detail from the memory they used in this lesson, such as the smooth glass of a window or the texture of a piece of clothing. Discuss the emotion this detail evokes. Compare and contrast the ways this emotion could be expressed in art, theatre, music, and dance.

Standards

National Theatre Standard: The student demonstrates acting skills (such as sensory recall, concentration, breath control, diction, body alignment, control of isolated body parts) to develop characterizations that suggest artistic choices.

Listening/Speaking Standard: The student follows verbal directions.

Reading/Variety of Texts Standard: The student reads widely for different purposes in varied sources. The student is expected to read classic and contemporary works.

Lesson **3**

Internal Characterization

Focus

Time: About 10 minutes

"In this lesson we will use emotional recall to experience a character's feelings." (*See page T16 for more about Emotional Recall.*)

Activate Prior Knowledge

▶ Hand out the **"Internal Characterization" Warm-Up,** and have students read the poem.

▶ Say, "This poem's speaker will be content with the person he or she loves as long as he or she doesn't travel. However, if the speaker travels and sees new things, it might become impossible to be content." Explain that sometimes an actor may use emotional recall if he or she is having trouble identifying with a character; for example, an actor who hates traveling might not identify with this poem.

Teach

Time: About 15 minutes

Prepare Have students remain in their seats.

Lead

▶ Have students close their eyes. Ask them to think of a time when they had a sudden, happy surprise. Tell them to remember every detail: the smells, the colors, and so on. Ask questions such as, "Was it hot or cold?"

▶ Say, "If some part of that memory made you feel excited again, you could use it to help you identify with, for example, a lost character who finds a path." If time allows, divide students into small groups and have them improvise a short scene in which all characters experience this emotion.

Informal Assessment Did students focus on the exercise?

History and Culture

Explain that emotional recall is ... This acting style was recorded by the Russian di... Stanislavsky in the early 1900s; he believed actors should ... emotions. Ask students for examples of actors ... plays whose emotions seemed faked. How did that affect the play or movie?

Reflect

Time: About 5 minutes

▶ Have students identify emotions the exercise evoked.

Apply

Journal: Describing

Have students suggest other characters in unusual situations. In their journals, have them describe a memory they could use to help them identify with one of the character's situations.

Name _____ Date _____

Internal Characterization

Why does the speaker in the poem want to travel? Where does the speaker in the poem want to go?

To the Not Impossible Him

by Edna St. Vincent Millay

How shall I know, unless I go
To Cairo and Cathay,
Whether or not this blessed spot
Is blest in every way?

Now it may be, the flower for me
Is this beneath my nose;
How shall I tell, unless I smell
The Carthaginian rose?

The fabric of my faithful love
No power shall dim or ravel
Whilst I stay here, —but oh, my dear,
If I should ever travel!

Objectives

Perception To identify ways to build a character externally

Creative Expression To use pantomime to portray physical traits of a character

History and Culture To contrast internal and external characterization

Evaluation To informally evaluate one's own work

Materials

- Copies of **"External Characterization" Warm-Up,** p. 43
- Journals or writing paper

Vocabulary

physicality

Standards

National Theatre Standard: The student demonstrates acting skills (such as sensory recall, concentration, breath control, diction, body alignment, control of isolated body parts) to develop characterizations that suggest artistic choices.

Listening/Speaking Standard: The student listens and uses information gained for a variety of purposes, such as gaining information from interviews, following directions, and pursuing a personal interest.

Writing Standard: The student is expected to write to express, discover, record, develop, reflect in ideas, and to problem solve.

 Lesson 4

External Characterization

Focus

Time: About 10 minutes

"In this lesson we will use pantomime to show characters." *(See page T3 for more about Pantomime.)*

Activate Prior Knowledge

▶ Distribute the **"External Characterization" Warm-Up,** and have students complete it.

▶ Discuss ways these details could help students act as Rosita. Explain that many actors build characters through observation and physicality, a focus on physical movement.

Teach

Time: About 15 minutes

Prepare Divide students into pairs. Have them clear an area.

Lead

▶ Have each pair divide the roles of Ramón and Rosita. Instruct them to move silently while focusing on safe physicality to show the characters. Encourage them to add details not described in the story.

▶ Have pairs proceed until you say, "Freeze." At that signal, tell them to stop, reverse roles, and repeat the movement exercise. Have volunteers share their movements with the class.

Informal Assessment Did each student safely use physicality?

 History and Culture

Explain that while some actors develop characters by working to experience these characters' thoughts and feelings, Representational actors work to represent a character's thoughts and feelings through careful movement and costume choices. Many actors combine several techniques.

Reflect

Time: About 5 minutes

▶ Have students develop criteria for critiquing this exercise based on their focus (physicality). Have them use these criteria to evaluate themselves. How could they improve?

Apply

Journal: Empathizing

Tell students that theatre involves both empathy, or identification with characters, and aesthetic distance, or an understanding that drama is not real life. Have students write journal entries describing movement that an actor could use to sensitively suggest a person recovering from a serious illness.

External Characterization

Read the passage below. It is a description of a child taking her first steps. Underline any words and phrases that help you see the movements the child and her father made.

Rosita was just ten months old when she started to walk. For weeks she had been pulling herself up by holding on to low tables and chairs. It was just a matter of time before she began to walk. Her dad Ramón took her out of the playpen, and she immediately crawled over to the coffee table and pulled herself up easily. Ramón came over and faced Rosita. He leaned over and took the child's hands in his to support her so she did not have to lean against the table anymore.

Ramón shuffled his left foot back a tiny bit to see what would happen. He was ready to catch Rosita, but that was not necessary. The baby's right foot moved forward, and she planted it hard. A big smile spread over Rosita's face. It was as if she were saying, "This is fun." As Ramón watched, her left foot moved forward. When it came down, it was not quite as far forward as her right foot. That was good because it helped the baby keep her balance. This success brought a squeal of laughter from Rosita. Her body wobbled back and forth a little.

Ramón carefully let go of Rosita's hand, got down on his knees, and moved a foot away from her. He held out his hands, always watchful to make sure she did not fall. He wanted Rosita's first "walking experience" to be a good one. Again, one chubby little foot moved forward followed by the other one. Rosita's head bobbed forward and she squealed as she reached Ramón. It was hard to tell who was more delighted. Ramón gently lowered his daughter into a sitting position and gave her a big hug.

Objectives

 Perception To identify a problem certain characters faced

 Creative Expression To use improvisation to solve a problem as a group

History and Culture To learn about the origins of theatre

Evaluation To informally evaluate one's own work

Materials

- Copies of **"Characters Solve a Problem" Warm-Up,** p. 45
- Scarf or hat
- Journals or writing paper

Standards

National Theatre Standard: The student acts in an ensemble, interacting as the invented characters.

Listening/Speaking Standard: The student listens, enjoys, and appreciates spoken language. The student is expected to listen to proficient, fluid models of oral reading, including selections from classic and contemporary works.

Reading Standard: The student is expected to read classic and contemporary works.

Lesson 5 Characters Solve a Problem

Focus

Time: About 10 minutes

"In this lesson we will improvise characters who work together to solve a problem." *(See page T4 for more about Improvisation.)*

Activate Prior Knowledge

▶ Distribute the **"Characters Solve a Problem" Warm-Up.** Read the poem aloud, but have two volunteers read the poem's first nine words and the words on the pedestal. Discuss Ozymandias's personality. *(powerful, proud, arrogant)* What problems might he have caused for his subjects?

Teach

Time: About 15 minutes

Prepare Divide students into groups of four.

Lead Show students a scarf or hat; when you put this on, you will become the leader of a secret council of citizens from Ozymandias's kingdom; each group will be council members. Put on the object.

▶ Say, "I have called this emergency meeting to discuss the problem of Ozymandias. We all know he has been an intolerable king. Could each group come up with three suggestions for a peaceful solution?" Give groups four or five minutes and, in role, visit each group.

▶ Have volunteers share suggestions. Have the class choose one suggestion, and have everyone participate in an improvisation of the suggestion—if necessary, you should act in the role of Ozymandias, stepping out of the role of leader by removing the scarf or hat.

Informal Assessment Did each student stay in character?

 History and Culture

Explain that some anthropologists believe theatre's beginnings can be found in ancient societies' rituals. Ceremonies in ancient Greece and India led to theatre performed for entertainment. Compare the role of theatre in these ancient societies with the roles of television, live theatre, film, and electronic media today. Have students research ancient Greek acting and improvise their problem-solving situation again, incorporating one element from this ancient style.

Reflect

Time: About 5 minutes

▶ Discuss the improvisation. What did the students learn about discussing solutions versus physically exploring them?

Apply

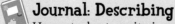 **Journal: Describing**

Have students write journal entries in which they describe the way one group of characters from books or movies worked together to solve a problem.

Characters Solve a Problem

Ozymandias

by Percy Bysshe Shelley

I met a traveller from an ancient land

Who said: Two vast and trunkless legs of stone

Stand in the desert. Near them on the sand

Half sunk, a shatter'd visage lies, whose frown

And wrinkled lip and sneer of cold command

Tell that its sculptor well those passions read

Which yet survive, stamp'd on these lifeless things,

The hand that mock'd them and the heart that fed;

And on the pedestal these words appear:

"My name is Ozymandias, king of kings:

Look on my works, ye Mighty and despair!"

Nothing beside remains. Round the decay

Of that colossal wreck, boundless and bare,

The lone and level sands stretch far away.

My name is Ozymandias,
king of kings:
Look on my works,
ye mighty and despair!

Objectives

Perception To review concepts about character and relate this information to real-life relationships

Creative Expression To write and perform a character monologue

History and Culture To research the ancient Incans and archaeology and connect this research to the character monologue

Evaluation To thoughtfully and honestly evaluate one's own participation using the four steps of criticism

Materials

- Copies of "Museum Announces Important Archaeological Find," p. 127

- Copies of the **Unit 2 Self-Criticism Questions,** p. 50

- Copies of the **Unit 2 Quick Quiz,** p. 51

- *Artsource®* Performing Arts Resource Package (optional)

Standards

National Theatre Standard: The student researches by using cultural and historical information to support improvised and scripted scenes. The student applies research from print and non-print sources to script writing, acting, design, and directing choices.

Lesson 6
Unit Activity: Scripted Monologue

Focus
Time: About 10 minutes

Review Unit Concepts

"Characters are people or sometimes personified animals or objects in a story or play. The main character, or protagonist, has a goal to achieve; the antagonist creates obstacles to this goal. Actors think about a character's motivations, sensory and emotional experiences, physical life, and relationships when building a character." **"Los personajes son personas o a veces animales personificados u objetos en una historia o drama. El personaje principal o protagonista tiene una meta que lograr; el antagonista crea obstáculos para esta meta. Los actores piensan en las motivaciones, las experiencias sensoriales y emocionales, vida física y relaciones de un personaje cuando desarrollan un personaje."**

► Review with students the ways in which they explored different aspects of characterization.

► Review the unit vocabulary on page 34.

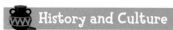 **History and Culture**

Explain that archaeological studies are carried on in many parts of the world where ancient civilizations existed. Have a group of students investigate the Incan civilization; have another group investigate what an archaeological dig site is like and some of the procedures that would have been followed by Dr. Gallardo, Nadia, and others working at the Peruvian site. Ask groups to report their findings to the class, and discuss how these findings could affect the students' monologues.

Classroom Management Tips

The following are tips for managing your classroom during the **Rehearsals** and **Activity:**

✔ **Set Ground Rules** You may wish to establish a signal, which will call the groups to attention. This signal could be a whistle or a physical symbol such as raising your hand.

✔ **Encourage Creativity** During the **First Rehearsal,** compliment students who came up with original questions or responses, especially those who suggested intriguing details to account for who Nadia is and why she responds as she does.

✔ **Provide Support** During the **Second Rehearsal,** encourage students to write down their monologue. Suggest that students experiment with tone of voice, attitude, and body language to support the character of Nadia that they have created.

Teach

Time: Two 15-minute rehearsal periods
One 15-minute activity period

First Rehearsal

▶ Distribute copies of **"Museum Announces Important Archaeological Find"** on page 127. Emphasize that they should note any details and information in the introduction. Have students read the article.

▶ Divide students into groups of three. Instruct each group to take notes about the character of Nadia Gallardo using the facts in the article as one source of information. Explain that actors often create imaginary back stories for their characters that help make these characters seem more real. Tell students that their focus should be to identify Nadia's thoughts, feelings, and relationships, to creatively invent her objective and motivations, and to decide how she might react to the situation described in the article.

Second Rehearsal

▶ Have students stand up, get into their groups from the **First Rehearsal,** and locate their group notes.

▶ Say, "Today you will use your notes to write a monologue, or lines Nadia might say when describing the events from the article to a good friend of hers. Have her describe a problem she had to overcome during the excavation, such as the statue being lodged beneath a huge boulder." *(See page T10 for more about Script Writing.)*

▶ At some point, instruct the groups to have group members take turns reading their monologue to the group. Tell students to use emotional and sensory recall to develop their characterizations of Nadia. Remind them to select movement and speech based on their characterizations.

▶ Tell the groups to make revisions. Have them select one member to perform their monologue in the final session of this activity.

Character Activity

▶ Have students re-form their groups from the **Second Rehearsal.** Provide an area from which the monologues will be delivered.

▶ Have students identify appropriate audience behavior, and have them agree to apply it. Say, "The most important thing in this activity is for each actor to move and speak as Nadia and for the audience to get a grasp of who each group thinks Nadia really is."

▶ Have the designated member from each group deliver the group's monologue. Have students analyze their behavior as an audience. Discuss similarities and differences in the interpretations of Nadia.

Standards

National Theatre Standard: The student individually and in groups creates characters, environments, and actions that create tension and suspense. The student analyzes, evaluates, and constructs meaning from improvised and scripted scenes and from theatre, film, television, and electronic media productions.

Unit Links

Visual Arts: Color

Compare and contrast the use of color to communicate emotion in art and theatre. Tell students that, just as a visual artist may use color to show a feeling, costume designers may choose specific colors for costumes in order to project a character's emotional state. A striking real-life example of clothing color matching an emotional state comes from Victorian England. Because Queen Victoria dressed in black for decades in mourning for her husband, British women wore black for extended periods of time after a family member died. Compare and contrast ways music or dance could communicate mourning. Play some sad music and have students use it to dictate a character's mournful movements.

Theatrical Arts Connection

Television Discuss differences between how an actor seems in interviews and how an actor may be in real life, identifying his or her "public persona" as a possible type of character. What roles do television and television actors play in American society?

Film/Video Ask, "Who is responsible for creating characters people care about?" *(actor, actress, writer, director)* Discuss film characters that students have cared about but not necessarily liked. How do people's ideas of interesting characters reflect the role of film in American society?

Standards

National Theatre Standard: The student describes characteristics and compares the presentation of characters, environments, and actions in theatre, musical theatre, dramatic media, dance, and visual arts.

Reflect

Time: About 10 minutes

Assessment

▶ Have students evaluate their participation by completing the **Unit 2 Self-Criticism Questions** on page 50.

▶ Use the assessment rubric to evaluate the students' participation in the **Unit Activity** and to assess their understanding of character.

▶ Have students complete the **Unit 2 Quick Quiz** on page 51.

	3 Points	2 Points	1 Point
Perception	Gives full attention to review. Masters an understanding of the ways in which characters help or hinder each other and can connect this to relationships in real life.	Gives partial attention to review. Is developing an understanding of how characters help or hinder each other but cannot connect this to relationships in real life.	Gives little attention to review of unit concepts and vocabulary words. Has a minimal understanding of ways in which characters help or hinder each other and cannot connect this to relationships in real life.
Creative Expression	Exhibits a clear understanding of ways to build character as evidenced by the creation and dramatization of a realistic character monologue.	Exhibits a developing understanding of ways to build character as evidenced by an attempt to create and dramatize a character monologue that is somewhat realistic.	Exhibits a minimal understanding of ways to build a character as evidenced by poor participation in the creation and dramatization of a realistic character.
History and Culture	Fully participates in researching the Incan civilization or an archaeological dig site. Clearly connects details of this information to the **Activity.**	Shows moderate participation in researching the Incan civilization or an archaeological dig site. Can connect some detail of this information to the **Activity.**	Exhibits poor participation in researching the Incan civilization or an archaeological dig site. Cannot connect this information to the **Activity.**
Evaluation	Thoughtfully and honestly evaluates own participation using the four steps of art criticism.	Attempts to evaluate own participation, but shows an incomplete understanding of evaluation criteria.	Makes a minimal attempt to evaluate own participation.

Apply

▶ Ask students, "Do people in real life encounter obstacles as they pursue their hopes and dreams? *(yes)* Think of a dream or goal you have. Is there a person or force operating as an antagonist in the situation? Do you have any internal obstacles? How might the situation get worked out?"

▶ Brainstorm with students some situations in which problem solving might be used to overcome another person's antagonistic behavior in order to progress toward an identified goal.

View a Performance

Character in Theatre

▶ Have students analyze elements of appropriate audience behavior when viewing a performance, including respectful silence and attention. Have them agree to apply this behavior during the performance.

▶ If you have the *Artsource*® videocassette or DVD, have students view "The Mask Messenger" performed by Robert Faust, founder of *Faustwork Mask Theater*.

▶ Have students discuss and write answers to the following questions:

Describe What masks does Robert Faust wear? *(A small, gnome-like mask, a big mask with a confused expression, and so on.)*

Analyze How does he use physicality to become a character while wearing each mask? *(He bends his head and raises his shoulders to look like an ogre; he crawls around to become a fantastic creature, and so on.)*

Interpret Compare and contrast Robert Faust's movements with the movements you or a group member used when improvising or performing your monologue. How are his movements and your movements like or unlike movement in dance?

Decide How do you think each character's voice would have sounded? Why?

"Drama is powerful because its unique balance of thought and feeling makes learning enjoyable, exciting, challenging, and relevant to real-life concerns."

—Betty Jane Wagner,
professor/authority on educational drama

LEARN ABOUT
CAREERS IN THEATRE

Explain to students that costumes help establish a character's time and place, a character's relationships, and a character's economic status, age, and occupation, as well as his or her emotional state. Costume designers working in professional theatre oversee the work of the people who actually create the costumes. Discuss similarities and differences between scenic designers and costume designers. Have students imagine that they are costume designers. What kind of costume would be appropriate for Nadia? *(Answers should reflect the character's age and situation.)* Have students investigate the training necessary to become a costume designer and report their findings to the class. Compare the role of the costume designer with the role of a scenic designer (described in **Unit 1**).

Standards

National Theatre Standard: The student explains the knowledge, skills, and discipline needed to pursue careers and vocational opportunities in theatre, film, television, and electronic media.

Name _____   Date _____

Unit 2 Self-Criticism Questions

Think about how you contributed to the writing and performance of the monologue. Then answer the questions below.

1. **Describe** What things did you say and do in discussions that contributed to the building of the character of Nadia?

_____

_____

_____

2. **Analyze** How did your tone of voice and physicality as you improvised or performed the monologue add dimension to the character?

_____

_____

_____

3. **Interpret** How are you like and unlike the character of Nadia? Was it easy or hard build this character? Why?

_____

_____

_____

4. **Decide** If you could do this activity again, would you change anything you did? Why or why not?

_____

_____

_____

Name _____ Date _____

Unit 2 Quick Quiz

Completely fill in the bubble of the best answer for each question below.

1. A character is
- (A) a necessary part of theatre.
- (B) a person, personified animal, or personified object in a play or story.
- (C) developed by actors in many ways.
- (D) all of the above.

2. Actors do *not* usually build characters by
- (F) observing how the character interrelates with other characters.
- (G) experimenting with ways a character might move.
- (H) ignoring a character's motivations.
- (J) using recall techniques to understand a character's experiences or emotions.

3. The antagonist in a play or story is the character who
- (A) is trying to achieve a goal or dream.
- (B) offers advice and help to other characters.
- (C) has the smallest role.
- (D) creates obstacles for another character.

4. Which sentence is true?
- (F) All characters are called protagonists in a story or play.
- (G) Characters can be built both internally and externally.
- (H) A character's motivations do not relate to his or her objectives.
- (J) A protagonist usually does not have a dream or goal.

5. An objective is
- (A) a character's style of clothing.
- (B) the main character in a play.
- (C) the goal of a character in a play.
- (D) another word for an antagonist.

6. A motivation is
- (F) a character's reason for speech, feeling, and action.
- (G) the name for a special kind of movement.
- (H) something a character does that does not relate to an objective.
- (J) all of the above.

Score _____ (Top Score 6)

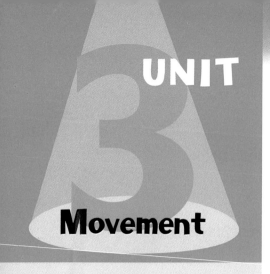

UNIT 3

Movement

Introduce Unit Concepts

"Movement can communicate a character's emotions, personality, age, and occupation. Actors and directors must make decisions about how movement will be used in a theatrical production. Sometimes actors use abstract movement to express concepts or ideas." *"El movimiento puede comunicar las emociones, personalidad, edad y ocupación de un personaje. Actores y directores tienen que tomar decisiones sobre cómo se usará el movimiento en una producción teatral. A veces los actores usan movimiento abstracto para expresar conceptos o ideas."*

Unit Overview

Lesson 1 • Movement and Emotion Characters can express emotion through movement and facial expressions. *Dramatic Movement*

Lesson 2 • Movement Communicates Silent movements can communicate elements of plot and character. *Pantomime*

Lesson 3 • Abstract Movement Actors can use movement to embody abstract concepts such as emotion. *Creative Movement*

Lesson 4 • Action, Reaction, and Inaction Physical actions, reactions, and inactions are part of actors interacting onstage. *Improvisation*

Lesson 5 • Rhythm and Repetition Characters have personal rhythms that may be expressed through repetitive movement. *Dramatic Movement*

Lesson 6 • Unit Activity: Dramatized Literary Selection This activity will give students the opportunity to plan and perform a pantomime.

See pages T3–T20 for more about **Theatre Technique Tips.**

Movement

▶ Have students brainstorm ways that age and occupation affect movement. *(Babies may not walk; many athletes can move quickly.)*

▶ Have students explore rhythm by pantomiming an ordinary, repetitive task, such as cleaning a room. Set their pace by tapping a pencil.

Vocabulary

Discuss the following vocabulary words.

abstract movement movimiento abstracto—a movement style in which emotions and ideas are evoked through nonrealistic, expressive motion

rhythm ritmo—an orderly or irregular pattern of movements; the speed and pace of an individual character or of a play as a whole

Unit Links

Visual Arts: Rhythm, Movement, and Pattern

▶ Tell students that visual rhythm in artwork creates the illusion of movement. Artists use rhythm to organize elements such as color or shape by repeating them; rhythm moves a viewer's eye through artwork. In music, rhythm is created by the duration of and pauses between musical sounds. Have students compare and contrast movement in art and music with actors' movement onstage. How does each communicate emotions and ideas? How do they affect the viewer or listener?

▶ Show students the image of a painting with visual rhythm, such as *Chinese Restaurant* by Max Weber. If you wish, have students respond to the image using movement, possibly by creating the movement of a busy restaurant while music with a frantic pace is played.

Reading Theme: Taking a Stand

▶ Discuss how the following applies to someone who takes a stand against wrongdoing: "The only place to find courage is within oneself."

▶ Ask students to think about the statement above in the context of their own lives. Discuss situations in which taking a stand may be required.

Teacher Background

Background on Movement

Movement onstage serves many purposes. Actors use movement to communicate reactions and to express thoughts and feelings. Movement onstage also contributes to the rhythm of a character within a play and a play itself. Characters have different personal rhythms based on age, occupation, or mood. A director, along with actors, must work to synthesize character rhythms with the overall rhythm of a play.

Background on Acting

When actors use pantomime, they must place their focus on nonverbal communication. Their movements, gestures, and facial expressions must communicate information such as who characters are, where they are, what they are doing. Much of this unit is devoted to techniques that actors use to explore and perfect ways to portray a character physically.

Research in Theatre Education

"Through classroom theatre, however, new reading resources became available to these ["at-risk"] children . . . [they] expanded their understandings and explored alternative expressions; they began to see themselves as actors, as *expressers,* and for the first time, the author concludes, as *readers.*"

—James S. Catterall

on "The Flight of Reading: Shifts in Instruction, Orchestration, and Attitudes through Classroom Theatre" in *Critical Links*

Differentiated Instruction

Reteach
Show students a muted scene from a video or a television program with which they are not familiar. Discuss examples of the following: action, reactions, and inaction; communication of emotion and attitude; and patterns of rhythm and repetition.

Challenge
Have students select a short scene from a favorite book or story and enact it in pantomime for the class. Suggest that in addition to the actors, they appoint a sound designer to create sound effects.

Special Needs
The 1960s Civil Rights movements addressed oppression faced by many groups of people. Use Lesson 1 as an opportunity to foster disability awareness by having students explore the reasons that persons with disabilities were engaged in protest.

Theatre's Effects Across the Curriculum

★ **Reading/Writing**
  Reading Response Reading a script and then analyzing its nonverbal aspects through pantomime and improvisation is another way to practice interpreting a written text.

★ **Math**
  Identifying Patterns Students create and manipulate visual patterns and then transform those patterns into dramatic movement

★ **Science**
  Force and Motion Students' activities exploring how the body moves when pushing against a heavy object are another way to understand the relationship between force and motion.

★ **Social Studies**
  History Students draw parallels between cause-and-effect relationships that exist in dramatic movement and cause-and-effect relationships within historical events.

★ **Music**
  Communication Rhythmic music compels students to move and to feel emotions; when this is used in theatre it provides a strong motivation and lends support for the actors.

★ **Dance**
  Abstract Movement Actors use abstract gestures to express emotion and environmental factors; students can use these gestures as movement themes to develop into dance combinations and phrases.

Objectives

 Perception To discern the emotions of characters from their nonverbal communication

 Creative Expression To express emotion using dramatic movement

 History and Culture To learn about *Noh* theatre, a type of Japanese drama

Evaluation To informally evaluate one's own work

Materials

📄 Copies of "Movement and Emotion" Warm-Up, p. 55

⭕ Journals or writing paper

Standards

National Theatre Standard: The student articulates and supports the meanings constructed from theirs and others' dramatic performances .

Listening/Speaking Standard: The student participates in classroom discussions using effective speaking strategies (for example, asking questions, making observations).

Reading/Comprehension Standard: The student is expected to offer observations, make connections, react, speculate, interpret, and raise questions in response to texts.

 Lesson 1

Movement and Emotion

Focus

Time: About 10 minutes

"In this lesson we will use dramatic movement to show characters and their emotions." *(See page T13 for more about Dramatic Movement.)*

Activate Prior Knowledge

▶ Hand out the **"Movement and Emotion" Warm-Up,** and have students read the story. Discuss how movement added to the suspense of the story. What emotions did Bianca experience?

Teach

Time: About 15 minutes

Prepare Divide students into three groups.

Lead Explain that they will show one action taken by characters who are motivated by injustice. Suggest groups from history and heritage such as nonviolent protestors in the 1960s Civil Rights movement.

▶ Give groups time to plan. Encourage students to think about how each character might feel in this situation and to safely use their entire bodies when moving as these characters. Tell them to think about people they have observed in real life.

▶ Have volunteers share their dramatic movements with the class. If time allows, have students replay and add dialogue.

Informal Assessment Did each student participate and use safe dramatic movement to express emotion?

 History and Culture

Explain that *Noh* is a type of Japanese theatre that combines music, poetry, dance, and drama. The participants include actors, a chorus, and instrumentalists. Rather than seeking to seem like people in real life, Noh actors attempt to express characters' essences. Actors' gestures may have specific meaning or may communicate emotions. Select a movement from this lesson's exercise, and have students find ways to simplify this movement and make it more symbolic.

Reflect

Time: About 5 minutes

▶ Ask the groups how they used observations of people in real life. How could empathy help an actor create a character's movements?

Apply

 Journal: Personal Writing
Discuss ways culture affects the physical expression of emotion. Have students write journal entries describing a time when they felt they could not express an emotion, why they felt this way, and how it relates to movement in theatre.

Name _____   Date _____

Movement and Emotion

The story below is the strange tale of a young woman named Bianca who looked into her mirror one day and saw something she had never seen before. As you read, notice how details about movement add suspense to the story.

The Mirror

Bianca had a rectangular-shaped mirror that was propped up on the desk in her room. She could not remember where the mirror came from; it had just always been there. The mirror looked old, but the polished wood of its frame was beautiful. When she sat at her desk, she often looked up to see her own image staring back at her. She would smile at her reflection and go back to her work.

One day, as she was busy with a complicated math assignment, she happened to glance into the mirror. What she saw startled her and made her gasp in fear. Her image, which should have been staring back at her, was actually doing something different. The image was standing in front of a girl who was crying. Bianca recognized the girl—it was Laney Taylor. Bianca and her friends had teased Laney just yesterday. She had not wanted to, but her friends liked to make fun of Laney's shabby clothes.

Suddenly the image sensed that Bianca was watching. Slowly, it turned its head away from the window and toward Bianca so that it was staring right into her eyes. The image looked sad and disappointed. It shook its head.

Bianca blinked, and suddenly the image in the mirror was just a normal reflection again. When Bianca's hand moved, the image's hand moved. When Bianca picked up her pen, the image did the same thing. Everything seemed to be back to normal.

That very evening Bianca found a large cloth. She took it to her desk and, without looking into the mirror, wrapped it in the cloth. Then she took the wrapped mirror up into the attic. She never went near the mirror again. If the house is still standing, the mirror is probably still there in the attic, wrapped up in that cloth.

Lesson 2
Movement Communicates

Focus

Time: About 10 minutes

"In this lesson we will pantomime situations in which people have to take a stand." *(See page T3 for more about Pantomime.)*

Activate Prior Knowledge

▶ Hand out the **"Movement Communicates" Warm-Up,** and read it aloud while students follow along. Discuss any unfamiliar words.

▶ Say, "Imagine one of the writers was carrying the letter to the Union Convention. How might he or she move? What would it communicate?" Have students demonstrate different ways the letter writer might walk.

Teach

Time: About 15 minutes

Prepare Divide students into groups of three.

Lead Tell each group to think of a situation from their own lives in which, like the former slaves who wrote that letter, they or someone they know bravely chose to take a stand.

▶ Have each group choose one member's example and pantomime what might have happened if the person had not chosen to act, and then have them recreate the pantomime, showing the person taking a stand. Instruct them to use specific and safe movements. Give students a few minutes to plan.

▶ Have groups briefly perform their pantomimes for the class. Allow each group to explain and describe the characters, relationships, setting, and meaning of its pantomime.

Informal Assessment Did each student participate in the group's pantomime, using safe movements?

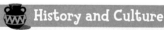

History and Culture

Tell students that in early silent films, actors could not rely on their voices and words to communicate, so they used exaggerated facial expressions and body language. Share examples of silent film performers, such as Lillian Gish and Charlie Chaplin, and, if possible, show clips from recordings of their films on videos or the Internet.

Reflect

Time: About 5 minutes

▶ Discuss what specific movements communicate.

Apply

Journal: Describing

Have students write a journal entry describing a real life situation in which it is more practical to communicate nonverbally than verbally, such as during a storm or in a factory.

Name _____ Date _____

Movement Communicates

We Claim Freedom

from *Black Residents of Nashville to the Union Convention,*
January 9, 1865 (Adapted)

In 1865, 59 former slaves from Nashville, Tennessee,
bravely wrote a letter to the men who were changing
the state constitution. They argued that slavery must
be outlawed, that African Americans deserve the right
to vote, and that they should be able to testify in court.

To the Union Convention of Tennessee Assembled
in the Capitol at Nashville, January 9th, 1865:

We the undersigned petitioners, American citizens of African descent, natives and residents of Tennessee, and devoted friends of the great National cause, do most respectfully ask a patient hearing of your honorable body in regard to matters deeply affecting the future condition of our unfortunate and long suffering race.

First of all, however, we would say that words are too weak to tell how grateful we are to the Federal Government for the good work of freedom which it is gradually carrying forward; and for the Emancipation Proclamation which has set free all the slaves in some of the rebellious States, as well as many of the slaves in Tennessee.

After 200 years of bondage and suffering a returning sense of justice has awakened the great body of the American people to make amends for the unprovoked wrongs committed against us for over 200 years.

Your petitioners would ask you to complete the work begun by the nation at large and abolish the last traces of slavery by the clear words of your law. Many masters in Tennessee whose slaves have left them will certainly make every effort to bring them back to bondage unless slavery be ended by the Constitution.

We claim freedom as our natural right, and ask that in harmony and cooperation with the nation at large, you should cut up by the roots the system of slavery, which is not only a wrong to us, but the source of all the evil which at present afflicts the State.

This is not a Democratic Government if a numerous, law-abiding, industrious, and useful class of citizens, born and bred on the soil, are to be treated as aliens and enemies, as an inferior degraded class, who must have no voice in the Government which they support, protect, and defend, with all their heart, soul, mind, and body, both in peace and war.

Objectives

Perception To define abstract movement

Creative Expression To use abstract movement to communicate a concept or idea

History and Culture To compare movement in dance and movement in drama

Evaluation To informally evaluate one's own work

Materials

- Copies of **"Abstract Movement"** Warm-Up, p. 59

- Sound objects such as a bell or pencil with which to tap

- Journals or writing paper

Vocabulary

realistic
abstract

Unit Links

Visual Arts: Movement
Like actors, artists create visual movement to communicate emotions and ideas. Have students compare and contrast realistic artwork, such as a work by Andrew Wyeth, with abstract or nonobjective art, such as one of Picasso's later works. Discuss reasons actors might use abstract movement or artists might create abstract art.

Standards

National Theatre Standard: The student expresses and compares personal reactions to several art forms.

Listening/Speaking Standard: The student is expected to present dramatic interpretations of experiences, stories, poems, or plays to communicate.

Science Standard: The student knows that there is a relationship between force and motion.

Lesson 3 # Abstract Movement

Focus
Time: About 10 minutes

"In this lesson we will use creative movement to show the concept of struggle." *(See page T12 for more about Creative Movement.)*

Activate Prior Knowledge

▶ Distribute the **"Abstract Movement" Warm-Up,** and have students read the passage. Have volunteers share their drawings.

▶ Say, "Sometimes actors use abstract movement to show an idea, such as *struggle* or *freedom.* Abstract movement uses aspects of dance; the actor uses his or her body creatively."

Teach
Time: About 15 minutes

Prepare Have students stand up and spread out around the room.

Lead Explain that each student will move safely to communicate the concept of *struggle.*

▶ As a starting point for their abstract movement, suggest that they think about how it feels to push against a very heavy object or move under gravity that is stronger than Earth's. Have students brainstorm how their drawings on the **Warm-Up** can help them think about *struggle.*

▶ Have all students simultaneously use abstract movement to show struggle while you tap a pencil or ring a bell to set the tempo of their movements. Side coach if needed, reminding them to show the concept rather than character actions.

Informal Assessment Did each student attempt to use safe, creative movement to show the concept of *struggle?*

History and Culture

Explain that movements in drama and in dance have many connections. Both can be a response to an external stimulus, such as music or sound, and both are avenues of non-verbal, self-expression. Discuss dances that students have seen, or show a video of dancers. Have students compare and contrast their abstract movements with the movements of dancers.

Reflect
Time: About 5 minutes

▶ Have students compare and contrast different movement choices.

Apply

Journal: Observing
Discuss ways actors can use real-life observations when creating many kinds of movement. Have students write a journal entry describing observations that could have helped them in the creative movement exercise.

Name _____ Date _____

Abstract Movement

Read the passage below, and then draw a person who illustrates or shows the idea of struggle.

"We must be the change we wish to see."—Mahatma Gandhi

It is not easy to work for change. Although many people have tried to work for peaceful change, they often face great danger from people who do not want change.

One way to seek peaceful change is through nonviolence. Mahatma Gandhi, a native of India, is known for using nonviolence in his quest to do away with unfair laws and customs in his native land of India and in South Africa. Gandhi believed that violence could never solve a conflict. Throughout his life, Gandhi fasted, or did not eat, to protest injustice. Dr. Martin Luther King, Jr., liked Gandhi's ideas and encouraged nonviolence in the American Civil Rights movement of the 1950s and 60s.

Nonviolence does not mean protection from danger. During one nonviolent protest, many of Gandhi's followers were killed in a walled-in area of the city of Amritsar. When African Americans in Alabama stopped riding the bus in protest of segregation, the police tried to stop those who carpooled together. Dr. King was put in jail many times and had bombs set in his house.

Working for change is sometimes a struggle, but it is important. Danger does not scare off people who truly want to see change.

Objectives

🔍 Perception To understand the relationship of action to reaction and inaction

🎨 Creative Expression To use improvisation as a context for understanding action, reaction, and inaction

🏺 History and Culture To learn how the tale of Scheherazade and other stories from *The Arabian Nights* have been interpreted

💬 Evaluation To informally evaluate one's own work

Materials

📄 Copies of "Action, Reaction, and Inaction" Warm-Up, p. 61

⭘ Journals or writing paper

Vocabulary

action
reaction
inaction

Standards

National Theatre Standard: The student, individually and in groups, creates characters, environments, and actions that create tension and suspense.

Listening/Speaking Standard: The student demonstrates nonverbal cues to convey a message to an audience (for example, movements, gestures, facial expressions).

Social Studies Standard: The student understands the relationship between artistic, creative, and literary expressions and societies that produce them.

Lesson 4 — Action, Reaction, and Inaction

Focus

Time: About 10 minutes

"In this lesson we will improvise actions, reactions, and inaction."
(See page T4 for more about Improvisation.)

Activate Prior Knowledge

▶ Hand out the **"Action, Reaction, and Inaction" Warm-Up,** and have students read the story. Tell students to underline actions that lead to or prevent other actions. Discuss student's examples.

▶ Have students share real-life examples of actions and reactions.

Teach

Time: About 15 minutes

Prepare Divide students into pairs. Have them spread out.

Lead Explain that each pair will improvise movements and words to demonstrate actions, reactions, and inaction in one of the following scenes: **(1)** Scheherazade convinces her father to allow her to marry the Sultan; **(2)** Scheherazade convinces her sister to help her outwit the Sultan; **(3)** Scheherazade tells her first story and stops the Sultan from killing her;

▶ Tell students that they may change reactions in their sections. Remind them to safely physicalize through facial expression and gesture. Allow one minute for planning.

▶ Have as many volunteers as possible improvise for the class.

Informal Assessment Did each pair work together to safely show actions and reactions in a scene from the story?

🏺 History and Culture

The Arabian Nights, the collection of folktales in which the story of Scheherazade is found, first appeared in Arabic around 850 A.D. Many of these folktales, such as "Ali Baba and the Forty Thieves" or "Aladdin," have been adapted for film, ballet, and musical composition. Explain that cultures often change stories to fit their cultural beliefs. What does this lesson's story tell us about the culture from which it comes? Would students change anything in a modern film version of it?

Reflect

Time: About 5 minutes

▶ Discuss ways in which students physicalized actions and reactions.

Apply

📓 Journal: Cause and Effect

Have students write journal entries comparing two historical events that caused reactions.

Name _____   Date _____

Action, Reaction, and Inaction

Scheherazade Tells a Story

an Iranian folktale, retold in *The Arabian Nights Entertainments,*
translated and edited by Andrew Lang (Adapted)

Long ago the Sultan Schahriar of Persia had a wife whom he loved more than anything, but because she betrayed him and broke his heart, he had her put to death. Schahriar declared that he was quite sure that all women were as wicked as the sultana. From then on, every evening he married a fresh wife and had her killed the following morning before the grand-vizir, whose duty it was to provide these unhappy brides.

The grand-vizir himself had two daughters, of whom the elder was called Scheherazade, and the younger Dinarzade. Scheherazade was very clever and courageous.

One day, when the grand-vizir was talking to her, Scheherazade said to him, "Father, I have a favor to ask of you. I must save the women from the awful fate that hangs over them. Allow me to be the Sultan's next wife." The grand-vizir was horrified, but Scheherazade kept asking until he finally gave way and went sadly to the palace.

Thanking her father, Scheherazade next spoke to her sister Dinarzade.

"My dear sister," Scheherazade said, "I need your help. I shall beg the Sultan to let you sleep in our chamber during the last night I am alive. If he grants me my wish, wake me an hour before the dawn, and say to me, 'My sister, if you are not asleep, I beg you to tell me one of your charming stories.'" Dinarzade agreed to do this.

Scheherazade asked the Sultan to allow her sister to be with her, and he granted her request. An hour before daybreak Dinarzade awoke, and asked her sister to tell one of her charming stories. "Will your highness permit me to do as my sister asks?" Scheherazade said to the Sultan.

"Willingly," he answered. So Scheherazade began to tell the most wonderful tale of the genius and the merchant. When it was almost day, she stopped speaking.

"I know you must attend your council," Scheherazade said to the sultan, "But if you would allow me to live another day, I will tell the rest of it to you the next night."

Schahriar said to himself, "I will wait till tomorrow; I can always have her killed when I have heard the end of her story."

The next night Sultan did not wait for Scheherazade to ask his permission.

"Finish," said he, "the story of the genius and the merchant. I am curious to hear the end."

So Scheherazade went on with the story. Every morning for one thousand and one nights, the Sultana told a story, and the Sultan let her live to finish it. At the end of these thousand and one nights, the Sultan's heart had softened. Scheherazade had saved the women of her country just as she had said.

Objectives

 Perception To understand the concepts of rhythm and repetition as they relate to movement

 Creative Expression To explore the personal rhythm of characters using dramatic movement and repetition

 History and Culture To learn about the nine areas of a theatre stage

 Evaluation To informally evaluate one's own work

Materials

📄 Copies of **"Rhythm and Repetition" Warm-Up,** p. 63

○ Tape or CD player and an audiocassette or CD with instrumental music that evokes a certain mood (optional)

○ Rattle or drum (optional)

○ Journals or writing paper

Vocabulary

rhythm
repetition

Standards

National Theatre Standard: The student incorporates elements of dance, music, and visual arts to express ideas and emotions in improvised and scripted scenes.

Listening/Speaking Standard: The student asks questions and makes comments and observations that reflect understanding and application of content, processes, and experiences.

Language Arts Standard: The student produces visual images, messages, and meanings that communicate with others.

Lesson 5

Rhythm and Repetition

Focus

Time: About 10 minutes

"In this lesson we will use dramatic movement to show a character's personal rhythm." *(See page T13 for more about Dramatic Movement.)*

Activate Prior Knowledge

▶ Hand out the **"Rhythm and Repetition" Warm-Up,** and have students complete it. Discuss the blocking plans.

▶ Say, "Rhythm can be a pattern of repeated motions, but in a play it can also mean the speed and changes of speed in a certain character's pattern of movement." Discuss factors that affect a character's rhythm, such as age or emotions.

Teach

Time: About 15 minutes

Prepare Have students create a simple set version of the **Warm-Up's** floor plan.

Lead Explain that, one at a time, each student will enter the set through the front door, sit on the couch, and stand and exit toward the kitchen. Each student should decide on a character's rhythm and pace based on age, personality, and emotions. They should create motivations for movement. Tell them to safely interact with the set.

▶ Allow time for planning. Have each student perform the actions on the set. If you wish, repeat this exercise, first playing music, such as a mournful instrumental piece, and then using a drum or rattle to set the students' pace. Have volunteers repeat their actions, changing their mood and pace to match the music and sounds.

Informal Assessment Did each student participate in the activity, attempt to safely move as a character, and apply audience behavior?

 History and Culture

Modern stages are often divided into sections to make communication easier. Write the following explanation on the board: *U*="Up," *R*="Right," *L*="Left;" *C*="Center," *D*="Down." Have volunteers name the nine stage areas from the **Warm-Up.** *(Up Right, and so on)* Note that left and right refer to an *actor's* left and right when facing the audience.

Reflect

Time: About 5 minutes

▶ Have students construct meaning from each other's movements.

Apply

 Journal: Comparing
Have students compare movement in film, television, and live theatre in their journals.

Name _____ Date _____

Rhythm and Repetition

Look at the sample and the floor plan for a play below. Imagine you are planning a character's movement, also called *blocking*. This character is nervously waiting for someone to arrive at the front door. Plan repeated movements for this character, using dotted lines and arrows as shown in the sample.

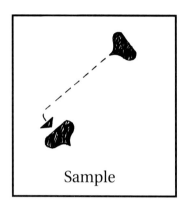

Sample

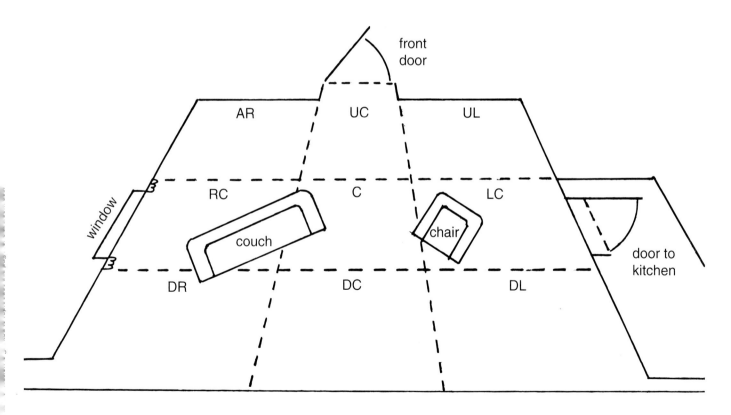

Objectives

 **Perception** To review drama concepts about movement and think about this information as it relates to communication and interactions in real life

Creative Expression
To dramatize a literary selection using pantomime

History and Culture
To research Henrik Ibsen, as well as real-life examples of severe pollution

Evaluation To thoughtfully and honestly evaluate own participation using the four steps of criticism

Materials

- Copies of "**Dr. Stockmann Takes a Stand**", pp. 128–131

- Audiocassette or CD player; recorded music to set the mood for the pantomime

- Copies of the **Unit 3 Self-Criticism Questions**, p. 68

- Copies of the **Unit 3 Quick Quiz**, p. 69

- *Artsource®* Performing Arts Resource Package (optional)

Standards

National Theatre Standard: The student describes and compares universal characters and situations in dramas from and about various cultures and historical periods, illustrates in improvised and scripted scenes, and discusses how theatre reflects a culture.

Lesson 6 Unit Activity: Dramatized Literary Selection

Focus

Time: About 10 minutes

Review Unit Concepts

"Movement helps tell the story of a play. It can show who a character is and how that character feels about other characters. Actors sometimes use abstract movement, which includes aspects of dance, to capture the essence of an idea. The movements or actions of a character affect other characters and cause reactions. A character has a personal rhythm; a play has an overall rhythm that affects an audience." "**Movimiento ayuda a contar la historia de un drama. Puede mostrar como realmente es un personaje y como ese personaje se siente sobre los demás personajes. Actores a veces usan movimientos abstractos, que incluyen aspectos de baile, para capturar la esencia de una idea. Los movimientos o acciones de un personaje afectan a los demás personajes y causan reacciones. Un personaje tiene un ritmo personal; un drama también tiene su propio ritmo que afecta a un público.**"

► Review with students the ways in which they explored different aspects of movement in theatre.

► Review the unit vocabulary on page 52.

History and Culture

To provide background for the **Activity,** have a group of students use research tools, including the Internet, to find out about Henrik Ibsen's life, his contribution to theatre, and how he attempted to take a stand against injustice through his writing. Have another group investigate real-life examples of modern people taking a stand against pollution. Have these students share their findings with the class. Have students write a paragraph using at least three supporting examples from the research to explain why stories about people taking a stand against injustice contain universal characters and themes.

Classroom Management Tips

The following are tips for managing your classroom during the **Rehearsals** and **Activity:**

✔ **Encourage Creativity** During the **Second Rehearsal,** encourage and compliment creative additions or adjustments in terms of characterization and in terms of the handling of real or imaginary props.

✔ **Take the First Risk** You may wish to take a role in the pantomime. It could be a central role through which you could help move the action along. Alternatively, you might choose to be part of the crowd to encourage students in this role to stay involved and to add status to their contributions.

Teach

Time: One 25-minute rehearsal period;
One 15-minute rehearsal period
One 20-minute activity period

First Rehearsal

► Distribute copies of **"Dr. Stockmann Takes a Stand"** on pages 128 through 131.

► Discuss briefly the format of a play script. Have the class read the play aloud with volunteers reading different parts. Discuss briefly the play's title and why Dr. Stockmann is considered to be the "enemy of the people."

► Tell students that they are going to plan to perform a pantomime of the events in "Dr. Stockmann Takes a Stand." *(See page T3 for more about Pantomime.)* Divide the class into two groups. Each group should select a note-taker and someone to report decisions. Give each group any time remaining to begin work on the following tasks:

Group 1: Choose visual elements and props, such as chairs, from the classroom and draw a diagram of the floor plan. Plan where the characters will sit and stand at the beginning of the pantomime.

Group 2: Study the script to locate any sound effects that might be needed. Choose a style of music to play during the pantomime, and have someone agree to provide a recording of the music.

► Have each group share any decisions they made.

Second Rehearsal

► Have students re-form their groups from the **First Rehearsal.** Give them time to finish and share their plans.

► Choose volunteers to play each of the parts, including non-speaking crowd members. You may wish to perform the role of Aslaksen as a way to exercise control during the pantomime and to rile up the crowd.

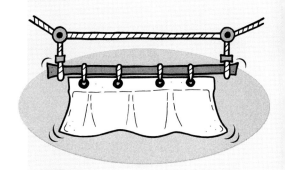

► Have students spread out around the room. Say, "How do you think your character feels before the town meeting. What kinds of repeated movements might he or she use? What is his or her personal rhythm?"

► Have all students act simultaneously to show their characters getting ready for the meeting. Tell them to use emotional and sense memory (covered in **Unit 2**) to help them identify with the characters.

Movement Activity

► Have Group 1 arrange the room and the actors for the beginning of the pantomime. Allow Group 2 to set up the music and any sound effects objects, such as a bell, to be used in the pantomime.

► Remind students to use not only facial expressions and gestures, but to safely use their whole bodies to communicate actions and reactions. Remind them to think about each character's personal rhythm as well as his or her actions and reactions to what happens. Instruct them to use the props and other visual elements safely.

► Perform the scene as a pantomime. If time allows, repeat the scene and have students add in the characters' speech from the scripts.

Standards

National Theatre Standard: The student leads small groups in planning visual and aural elements and in rehearsing improvised and scripted scenes, demonstrating social, group, and consensus skills. The student, individually and in groups, creates characters, environments, and actions that create tension and suspense.

Unit Links

Visual Arts: Rhythm, Movement, and Pattern

Both visual artists and actors express ideas and transform emotions. Remind students that a visual artist produces images using principles such as rhythm, movement, or pattern. The actor produces characters that move, speak, and react. Both often go through a process of research: planning; choosing and rejecting; and developing until they are satisfied with the completed product. Have students consider the ways other producers of art, such as authors, poets, dancers, and composers, use this same process to communicate.

Theatrical Arts Connection

Television Ask students to name some "action" shows they see on television. Discuss the distinctions between physical action that is largely combat and the spectrum of types of movement that reveal more about character. Discuss these actions in the context of television's role in American society.

Film/Video Show a video of clowns performing in a Cirque de Soleil performance, such as *Alegria*. Have students compare and contrast it with the performances of other types of more traditional clowns. If possible, invite a person in the community who does clowning to visit and be interviewed by interested students. What is the role of this type of theatre in American society? *(entertainment)*

Standards

National Theatre Standard: The student uses articulated criteria to describe, analyze, and constructively evaluate the perceived effectiveness of artistic choices found in dramatic performances.

Reflect

Time: About 10 minutes

Assessment

▶ Have students evaluate their participation by completing the **Unit 3 Self-Criticism Questions** on page 68.

▶ Use the assessment rubric to evaluate the students' participation in the **Unit Activity** and to assess their understanding of movement.

▶ Have students complete the **Unit 3 Quick Quiz** on page 69.

	3 Points	2 Points	1 Point
Perception	Gives full attention to review of unit concepts and vocabulary words. Masters movement concepts covered in this unit and can connect them to real-life character traits.	Gives partial attention to review of unit concepts and vocabulary words. Is developing an understanding of movement concepts, but has trouble connecting them in some way to real-life character traits.	Gives minimal attention to review of unit concepts and vocabulary words. Has a poor understanding of movement concepts covered in this unit and cannot connect them in some way to real-life character traits.
Creative Expression	Fully participates in the pantomime; works to fully portray all of the following through movement: a character's actions, reactions, and personality.	Partially participates in the pantomime; works to fully portray two of the following through movement: character's actions, reactions, and personality.	Shows poor participation in the pantomime; works to portray one of the following through movement: character's actions, reactions, and personality.
History and Culture	Writes a paragraph about the universality of the characters and the theme of the literary selection using three examples from the class research.	Writes a paragraph about the universality of the characters and the theme of the literary selection using two examples from the class research.	Writes a paragraph about the universality of the characters and the theme of the literary selection using one example from the class research.
Evaluation	Thoughtfully and honestly evaluates own participation using the four steps of art criticism.	Attempts to evaluate own participation, but shows an incomplete understanding of evaluation criteria.	Makes a poor attempt to evaluate own participation.

Apply

▶ Ask students, "In what way are the characters and theme, or main idea, of "Enemy of the People" like real-life people and situations? *(Some people are motivated by money, selfishness, and greed; some are motivated by honesty and values.)*

▶ Discuss historical people who each took a stand on an issue, even though their actions caused reactions such as anger, such as Sarah and Angelina Grimké, Martin Luther King, Jr., Karen Silkwood, Rachel Carson, Cynthia Cooper, Sherron Watkins, or Coleen Rowley. Have students choose one character trait these people shared, such as bravery, and have them use abstract movement to communicate that idea.

View a Performance

Movement in Dance

► Have students analyze the appropriate behavior that, as audience members, they should apply at every performance. Have students agree to apply this behavior.

► If you have the *Artsource®* videocassette or DVD, have students view "The Brass Ring," choreographed by Michael Tracy and performed by Pilobolus Dance Theatre. Alternatively, you may show them a video of a modern dance performance.

► Have students discuss and write answers to the following questions:

Describe What kinds of movements did the dancers use? *(slow, expressive movements, movements that seemed very deliberate)*

Analyze What kinds of characters or situations might these movements create? *(It seemed like two of the dancers were flying in space.)* What kind of mood did the music and dance create together? *(peaceful, thoughtful)*

Interpret Compare and contrast this dance with people's movement in real life. In what kinds of situations do people move slowly and deliberately? *(weddings, when they are sad, and so on)* Compare and contrast the way these dancers communicated ideas and feelings with the way actors, visual artists, and musicians communicate orally, aurally, visually, and through movement.

Decide Think about the movement you used in the activity and compare it with these dancers' movements. What did you like best about the dance?

```
"Physical actions are the necessary
balance for verbal actions. When the
actor is truly alive on the stage
there is an endless variety of
interaction between verbal and physical
behavior."

                          —Uta Hagen
             (1919- ), actress/writer
```

LEARN ABOUT CAREERS IN THEATRE

Say, "A stage manager contributes many things to the movement of actors and props. He or she is responsible for writing down blocking. The stage manager often helps the director and actors make decisions regarding where actors will start and how actors will move during each scene, and the stage manager keeps all that information in a notebook that is updated as necessary to reflect changes made. The stage manager is responsible for scheduling and sometimes helps the director stay focused." Explain that the stage manager has many more responsibilities including overseeing all technical aspects of a production. Have volunteers investigate the training that is necessary to become a stage manager and report their findings to the class. Compare this occupation to the occupation of an actor or director.

Standards

National Theatre Standard: The student explains the knowledge, skills, and discipline needed to pursue careers and vocational opportunities in theatre, film, television, and electronic media.

Name _____ Date _____

Unit 3 Self-Criticism Questions

Think about how you contributed to the pantomime of "Dr. Stockmann Takes a Stand." Then answer the questions below.

1. **Describe** What facial expressions, gestures, and other types of movement did you use to portray your character? If you replayed with sounds and dialogue, describe sounds and dialogue you used.

   _____

   _____

   _____

2. **Analyze** How would your actions express the events of the story and the emotions of your character to an audience?

   _____

   _____

   _____

3. **Interpret** Compare your performance with what you see, hear, say, and do at a dance or music performance or at an art show.

   _____

   _____

   _____

4. **Decide** If you could do this activity again, what would you change?

   _____

   _____

   _____

Name _____ Date _____

Unit 3 Quick Quiz

Completely fill in the bubble of the best answer for each question below.

1. **Movement is**
   - (A) something an audience sees onstage.
   - (B) a way to communicate with other actors and the audience.
   - (C) a way to develop character.
   - (D) all of the above.

2. **In pantomime, an actor**
   - (F) relies upon other actors to tell the story.
   - (G) projects his or her character through actions.
   - (H) works with a narrator to explain the action.
   - (J) gives long speeches.

3. **Actions**
   - (A) only create inaction.
   - (B) always introduce another character.
   - (C) often produce a reaction.
   - (D) never solve a problem.

4. **Which sentence is *not* true?**
   - (F) Words and movement are both important in theatre.
   - (G) An actor may use several techniques to create movement.
   - (H) A character's age does not affect how he or she moves.
   - (J) Movement can sometimes express what words cannot.

5. **Rhythm is**
   - (A) a pattern of movements.
   - (B) a character's speed and pace in a play.
   - (C) all of the above.
   - (D) none of the above.

6. **Blocking is**
   - (F) an actor's movements onstage.
   - (G) a special kind of costume.
   - (H) another name for a stage manager.
   - (J) only movement that involves picking up an object.

Score _____ (Top Score 6)

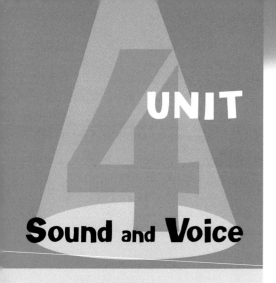

UNIT

4

Sound and Voice

Unit Overview

Lesson 1 • Sound and Silence Communicate Both sound and silence can communicate concrete and emotional information to an audience. *Sound Effects*

Lesson 2 • Music and Movement Music can help to set a mood. *Creative Movement*

Lesson 3 • Sound Creates a Setting Sound effects help communicate setting to an audience. *Sound Effects*

Lesson 4 • Character Voices Actors communicate character traits through character voices. *Storytelling*

Lesson 5 • Tone and Inflection Actors use tone and inflection to express the emotions, moods, and attitudes of characters. *Improvisation*

Lesson 6 • Unit Activity: Improvisation This activity will give students the opportunity to plan and perform an improvisation using sound effects.

See pages T3–T20 for more about **Theatre Technique Tips.**

Introduce Unit Concepts

"An audience's response to a play depends on what they hear as well as what they see. Sound effects, music, and the actors' voices provide this information." **"La reacción de un público a un drama depende tanto de lo que oye como de lo que ve. Efectos de sonido, música y las voces de los actores proporcionan esta información."**

Sound and Voice

▶ Ask, "How does the *way* a person says something affect his or her meaning?" *(If you say something kind in an unkind voice, it changes your meaning, and so on.)*

▶ Discuss information that sound communicates. What do specific styles of music make students think of? *(Jazz reminds me of New Orleans, and so on.)* Have students suggest sounds that evoke specific settings. *(Crickets chirping suggest night, and so on.)*

Vocabulary

Discuss the following vocabulary words.

tone tono—the use of inflection, or vocal pitch and volume, to communicate an emotional message

projection proyección—the use of vocal volume, clarity, and distinctness in order to be better heard by an audience

subtext subtexto—the character's inner feelings and intentions not expressed directly through dialogue

Unit Links

Visual Arts: Balance and Emphasis

▶ Tell students that balance is the principle of design that deals with the visual weight in a work of art; emphasis is used to draw attention to a certain area within a work of art. Compare and contrast the use of emphasis in art with the ways sound and voice can create emphasis in formal and informal theatre. *(They can draw attention to a particular character or area of the stage.)* How could a composer use emphasis in music? *(Certain notes could be louder than others, and so on.)*

▶ Show students the image of a portrait, such as *Self Portrait* by Rembrandt van Rijn. Discuss the use of balance and emphasis. Have students move and speak as Rembrandt based on the image.

Reading Theme: Beyond the Notes

▶ Have students list some of the places they hear music on a regular basis. What does the music in each place communicate?

▶ Ask students about the different ways that music is used in our culture. *(Music entertains; it sells things; it communicates ideas.)* How does music have meaning and influence in students' lives?

Teacher Background

Background on Sound and Voice

Actors use their voices as important tools for communication about and as characters. Sound effects can help an audience better imagine the setting, can motivate action onstage, and can help to create mood or atmosphere. Music, a specific subset of sound, may also be a part of a play's setting. Incidental music is played in the background of a scene, and it helps to establish the mood of a production.

Background on Sound Production

Sound designers and technicians who run sound are vital to most theatrical productions. When executed perfectly, sound effects and music powerfully enhance the story and performances. When execution is flawed, they can distract an audience and interfere with any attempts to suspend disbelief.

Research in Theatre Education

"De la Cruz's finding that drama training can improve the social skills of students with learning disabilities is a significant finding for a society concerned about the escalation of violence in schools and the need to balance pressures for accountability with realistic and effective approaches to the social development of students."

—Betty Jane Wagner

on "The Effects of Creative Drama on the Social and Oral Language Skills of Children with Learning Disabilities" in *Critical Links*

Differentiated Instruction

Reteach

Have students read a folktale or fable that includes animals as characters. Have students experiment with and plan character voices and sound effects. If possible have students dramatize the story for a class of young children.

Challenge

Have interested students create a selection of sound effects using a tape recorder. Have students organize their bank of sound effects into multiple categories.

Special Needs

Use the activities in this unit as an opportunity to develop interpersonal intelligence in all students. Being able to gather information from a person's tone, inflection, pauses, and body language are valuable relationship skills.

Theatre's Effects Across the Curriculum

★ **Reading/Writing**
   Reading Response Analyzing the dialogue in a story and portraying characters in storytelling and improvisation is another way to interpret written texts.

★ **Math**
   Predicting When students improvise scenes, they use character information to make predictions about the character's speech.

★ **Science**
   Observing Students must observe sounds in both outdoor and indoor environments in order to collect information useful in creating sound effects.

★ **Social Studies**
   Culture Students become aware of universal themes and character types when they learn about music from different cultures.

★ **Music**
   Pitch As students use different vocal pitches for characters, they are identifying a principle which is also used in opera, where heroes and heroines have higher voices, while the villains are played by singers with lower voices.

★ **Dance**
   Contrast As students experiment with degrees of sound and silence, they are exploring principles of contrast similar to those used in dances that incorporate both action and active stillness (energized held shapes or poses).

Sound and Silence Communicate

Objectives

 Perception To identify the use of onomatopoetic language in a poem

 Creative Expression To create sound effects to enhance an improvisation

 History and Culture To learn about the use of sounds effects during the golden age of radio

 Evaluation To informally evaluate one's own work

Materials

❍ A tape or CD player and a recording of an old radio program, such as *The Lone Ranger, Inner Sanctum,* or *The Shadow* (optional)

❍ Journals or writing paper

Vocabulary

sound effects
mood

Standards

National Theatre Standard: The student compares and incorporates art forms by analyzing methods of presentation and audience response for theatre, dramatic media (such as film, television, and electronic media), and other art forms.

Listening/Speaking Standard: The student is expected to listen to proficient, fluent models of oral reading, including selections from classic and contemporary works.

Writing Standard: The student is expected to write to express, discover, record, develop, reflect in ideas, and to problem solve.

Focus

Time: About 10 minutes

"In this lesson we will create sound effects to enhance an improvisation." *(See page T14 for more about Sound Effects.)*

Activate Prior Knowledge

▶ Read aloud **"Alarm Bells."** Define *onomatopoeia* as "words that both name and imitate sounds." Reread the poem; make a class list of onomatopoetic words from the poem. *(scream, shriek, clang, and so on)* Have students imitate and synthesize the sounds.

▶ Discuss the mood that the poem creates. *(tension, excitement)*

Teach

Time: About 15 minutes

Prepare Divide students into groups of four.

Lead Explain that students are going to safely use their voices to create sound effects for an improvised scene in which characters encounter a real-life problem.

▶ Have each group divide the roles of sound technicians and actors. Explain that actors will improvise scenes with actions that require sound effects, such as opening a car door, while the sound technicians will use their voices to create these sound effects. Allow time for planning.

▶ Have each group perform its brief improvisation. Have members switch roles so that each student has a turn creating sound effects.

Informal Assessment Did each student participate in the improvisation by acting and safely creating sound effects?

History and Culture

Explain that during the 1930s and 1940s, radio provided people with all types of entertainment. Sound technicians provided sound effects to help listeners imagine the action. If possible, share a recording of a radio drama with the class. Discuss the role of radio in this time period, and compare it with the roles of television, film, and live theatre today.

Reflect

Time: About 5 minutes

▶ Have students suggest ways in which they could improve their own performances and replay, incorporating suggestions.

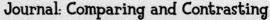

Apply

Journal: Comparing and Contrasting

In their journals, have students compare and contrast one sound effect they created with the actual sound in real life.

Alarm Bells

from "The Bells" by Edgar Allen Poe

Hear the loud alarum bells—

Brazen bells!

What a tale of terror, now, their
turbulency tells!

In the startled ear of night

How they scream out their affright!

Too much horrified to speak,

They can only shriek, shriek,

Out of tune,

In a clamorous appealing to the mercy
of the fire,

In a mad expostulation with the deaf and
frantic fire,

Leaping higher, higher, higher,

With a desperate desire,

And a resolute endeavor

Now—now to sit, or never,

By the side of the pale-faced moon.

Oh, the bells, bells, bells!

What a tale their terror tells

Of Despair!

How they clang, and clash, and roar!

What a horror they outpour

On the bosom of the palpitating air!

Yet the ear, it fully knows,

By the twanging

And the clanging,

How the danger ebbs and flows;

Yet the ear distinctly tells,

In the jangling

And the wrangling,

How the danger sinks and swells,

By the sinking or the swelling in the anger
of the bells—

Of the bells,—

Of the bells, bells, bells, bells,

Bells, bells, bells—

In the clamor and the clangor of the bells!

Objectives

 Perception To compare and contrast visual and kinesthetic responses to music

 Creative Expression To respond to music with creative movement

 History and Culture To learn about the use of music and dance in traditional American musical theatre

 Evaluation To informally evaluate one's own work

Materials

📄 Copies of **"Music and Movement" Warm-Up, p. 75**

○ Tape or CD player and recordings of several musical selections, two of which should suggest contrasting emotions, such as joy and sadness or hope and despair.

○ Video or DVD player and a recording of the movie *Oklahoma!* (optional)

○ Journals or writing paper

Vocabulary

subtext

Standards

National Theatre Standard: The student describes characteristics and compares the presentation of characters, environments, and actions in theatre, musical theatre, dramatic media, dance, and visual arts.

Listening/Speaking Standard: The student uses movement, placement, juxtaposition, gestures, silent periods, facial expressions, and other nonverbal cues to convey meaning to an audience.

Music Standard: The student is expected to describe aurally presented music representing diverse style, periods, and cultures.

Lesson 2 — Music and Movement

Focus

Time: About 10 minutes

"In this lesson we will use creative movement in response to music."
(See page T12 for more about Creative Movement.)

Activate Prior Knowledge

▶ Distribute the **"Music and Movement" Warm-Up.** Play each musical selection, and have students complete the **Warm-Up.**

▶ Play the selections again, and have students stand and move in response to the music. Have them compare and contrast how they expressed their responses visually and kinesthetically.

Teach

Time: About 15 minutes

Prepare Have students stand beside their desks.

Lead Tell students that you are going to play a new, short musical selection. Explain that they should identify how each selection makes them feel and then use their bodies to express that feeling.

▶ Play one short selection, providing time for students to respond with creative movement. Discuss the emotion(s) the music evoked in the students and analyze the various responses to it.

▶ Identify a situation whose mood matches the mood of the music. Have all students pantomime this situation while the music plays.

Informal Assessment Did each student respond to the music using creative movement and participate in the pantomime?

History and Culture

Tell students that in the 1930s and 1940s, music and dance became more closely aligned with plot and character development in musicals. For example, Agnes de Mille, choreographer of Rodgers and Hammerstein's 1943 production of *Oklahoma!* integrated music, song, and dance with both plot and character development. If possible show the "Dream Ballet" at the end of Act 1 in *Oklahoma!* Discuss how the dance and music show character subtext.

Reflect

Time: About 5 minutes

▶ Have students evaluate their movements, expressing personal preferences. Have them compare and contrast the creative movement with elements of dance.

Apply

📱 Journal: Describing
Have students write journal entries about experiences in which their lives were touched or changed by music.

Name _____ Date _____

Music and Movement

As you listen to two examples of music, use the boxes below to draw any lines, shapes, or other images in response to the music. Compare and contrast the drawings you create for each musical selection on the lines below.

First Musical Selection	Second Musical Selection

_____

_____

_____

_____

_____

_____

_____

_____

_____

_____

_____

Unit Links Reading: Beyond the Notes

Objectives

 **Perception** To understand how sound effects can suggest an environment

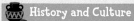 **Creative Expression** To establish a background environment to support a scene by means of sound effects

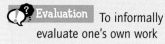 **History and Culture** To learn about the playwright Anton Chekhov and his use of sound effects

 Evaluation To informally evaluate one's own work

Materials

📄 Copies of **"Sound Creates a Setting" Warm-Up,** p. 77

⭕ Materials for sound effects creation, such as tissue paper, cellophane, small combs, paper clips, glasses, and small horns

⭕ Journals or writing paper

Unit Links

Visual Arts: Balance
Compare and contrast balance in visual art with balance in sound effects. Remind students that artists arrange elements in an artwork to create a sense of balance. Discuss the effect of sound effects being played from one side or both sides of a stage or from behind an audience. What does each communicate? Compare and contrast this with balanced musical amplification in rock concerts.

Standards

National Theatre Standard: The student works collaboratively and safely to create elements of scenery, properties, lighting, and sound to signify environments, and costumes and makeup to suggest character.

Listening/Speaking Standard: The student determines the purposes for listening, such as to gain information, to solve problems, or to enjoy and appreciate.

Social Studies Standard: The student explains the significance of individuals or groups from selected societies, past and present.

Lesson 3 Sound Creates a Setting

Focus

Time: About 10 minutes

"In this lesson we will create sound effects to show a setting." *(See page T14 for more about Sound Effects.)*

Activate Prior Knowledge

▶ Distribute the **"Sound Creates a Setting" Warm-Up,** and have students complete it.

▶ Discuss students' answers, and talk about the differences, benefits, and drawbacks of live and recorded sound effects.

Teach

Time: About 15 minutes

Prepare Divide students into groups of four.

Lead Explain that their objective will be to create sound effects using found objects, as well as their voices, hands, and feet, to create a specific setting for a scene. Have them choose one of the following settings: a beach on a beautiful day, the interior of a restaurant during lunch hour, an assembly line in a factory, or a street in a busy city.

▶ Circulate as students experiment, making suggestions if needed.

▶ Have each group demonstrate their sound effects to create a setting. Have the rest of the class try to identify what individual sounds represent.

Informal Assessment Did each student use available materials to create sounds for an environment?

History and Culture

Tell students that Anton Chekhov, a gifted Russian playwright and author born in 1860, regularly used sound effects to communicate setting and mood. For example, in his play *The Three Sisters* a sad farewell scene is underscored by the sounds of a distant, cheerful band. The contrast makes the mood seem even sadder. Brainstorm ways sound effects can contrast with and consequently emphasize a play's mood. Have students choose one group's sound effects and improvise a class scene in which the mood of the action contrasts with the mood of the sounds.

Reflect

Time: About 5 minutes

▶ Have each group evaluate its own performance and suggest ways they could improve next time.

Apply

Journal: Inferring

Before class locate a bank of appropriate, free sound effects on the Internet. Play several effects for the class without identifying them. Students should identify one of these sound effects and briefly describe in their journals a story or play in which this sound could be used.

Sound Creates a Setting

Imagine that you are a sound designer. It is your responsibility to provide sounds for a theatrical production. For the first scene of the first act, the director, based on suggestions from the playwright, wants you to create the sounds of a city park on a quiet summer evening. Beside each sound below, describe how you might create and record that sound effect, and how you would record any actual sounds in nature. For numbers 5 through 8, list other sound effects that would help to create this setting.

1. crickets chirping _____

_____

2. traffic somewhere in the distance _____

_____

3. children playing on the park playground _____

_____

4. a plane flying by _____

_____

5. _____

_____

6. _____

_____

7. _____

_____

8. _____

_____

Objectives

 Perception To understand the role of subtext in character speech

 Creative Expression To communicate subtext in storytelling

 History and Culture To identify, research, and compare universal animal characters in world folktales

 Evaluation To informally evaluate one's own work

Materials

📄 Copies of "Character Voices" Warm-Up, p. 79

○ Journals or writing paper

○ Video or DVD player and a recording of a cartoon film of your choice (optional)

Vocabulary

subtext

Standards

National Theatre Standard: The student analyzes description, dialogue, and actions to discover, articulate, and justify character motivation and invent character behaviors based on the observation of interactions, ethical choices, and emotional responses of people.

Listening/Speaking Standard: The student delivers narrative presentations using a range of narrative devices (e.g., dialogue, tension, or suspense).

Social Studies Standard: The student understands the similarities and differences within and among cultures in different societies.

Lesson 4 Character Voices

Focus

Time: About 10 minutes

"In this lesson we will tell stories and interpret their subtext." *(See page T11 for more about Storytelling.)*

Activate Prior Knowledge

▶ Say, "Sometimes the way a character speaks can reveal subtext, or information not directly spoken in the dialogue."

▶ Distribute the **"Character Voices" Warm-Up,** and have students read the folktale. Discuss each character's traits. *(Bluebird is honest and generous; Coyote is dishonest and proud.)* What truth did Coyote not speak during the story? *(He wanted to eat Bluebird.)*

Teach

Time: About 15 minutes

Prepare Divide students into pairs.

Lead Say "One member of each pair will act as Coyote and tell the story of 'Bluebird and Coyote.' Think about the dishonest and proud nature of Coyote and how he might retell this story in a way that makes him look better. Imagine that Coyote cannot blatantly *lie,* but he may color details or leave them out. The other member of each pair will explain the subtext of Coyote's speech for the class."

▶ Have each pair divide the roles of Coyote and subtext explainer, and have each pair briefly improvise for the class, allowing each Coyote actor to finish before the other student explains the subtext.

▶ Have each pair switch roles and repeat the improvised storytelling.

Informal Assessment Did each student tell the lesson's story as Coyote and explain subtext in another actor's speech?

 History and Culture

Explain that universal characters, such as the trouble-making trickster, are present in tales throughout the world. Bring in books of animal folktales from around the world. Have students compare Coyote or Wolf characters in several different cultures and how each animal's speech reveals character traits.

Reflect

Time: About 5 minutes

▶ Have students compare the use of subtext in the exercise with real life examples, such as a person saying "sorry," in an insincere manner.

Apply

📓 Journal: Comparing and Contrasting

Have students identify actors who provided character voices in animated movies, such as Eddie Murphy in *Shrek,* and, if possible, show an excerpt. Have students write journal entries comparing and contrasting how these actors used their voices to communicate subtext.

Name _____ Date _____

Character Voices

Bluebird and Coyote

a Cherokee tale

Long ago Bluebird's feathers were ugly and dull. Bluebird lived near a lake filled with blue water. The blue water did not change because no stream flowed into it and no stream flowed out of it. Bluebird liked the color of the water, so she washed in the lake four times a day for four days, and as she bathed she sang:

"There's blue water.

It lies there.

I went in.

I am blue."

On the fourth morning her ugly feathers fell off. On the fifth morning she came out with blue feathers.

Coyote had been watching Bluebird. He hoped to catch and eat Bluebird, but he was frightened by the blue water. On the fifth morning he said to Bluebird, "How is it that all your ugly color has come out of your feathers? You are all blue and lovely now. You are more beautiful than any bird of the air. I want to be blue too."

"I went in the lake four times," replied the Bluebird. She told Coyote the song she sang.

So Coyote jumped into the lake. For four mornings he did this, singing the song the Bluebird had taught him:

"There's blue water.

It lies there.

I went in.

I am blue."

On the fifth day he turned as blue as the bird.

Coyote was very proud. He strutted through the woods, looking to see if anyone was looking at his fine, blue coat.

He began to run, and as he ran he thought, "I wonder if my shadow is blue?" Coyote looked behind him to see if his shadow was blue too. He was so busy looking behind him that he did not see a tree ahead of him and he hit it hard. Coyote fell to the ground and became dust-colored. From that day to this, all coyotes are the color of the earth.

Unit Links Beyond the Notes

Objectives

 Perception To understand the concepts of tone and inflection as they relate to the voice

 Creative Expression To practice tone and inflection in dialogue using improvisation

 History and Culture To learn about how the playwright Harold Pinter used silence to communicate the subtext in his plays

 Evaluation To informally evaluate one's own work

Materials

🗐 Copies of **"Tone and Inflection" Warm-Up,** p. 81

○ Journals or writing paper

Vocabulary

tone
inflection
projection

Standards

National Theatre Standard: The student, in an ensemble, interacts as an invented character.

Listening/Speaking Standard: The student is expected to present dramatic interpretations of experiences, stories, poems, or plays to communicate.

Science Standard: The student is expected to collect data by observing and measuring.

Lesson 5 — Tone and Inflection

Focus

Time: About 10 minutes

"In this lesson we will use tone of voice in an improvised scene."
(See page T4 for more about Improvisation.)

Activate Prior Knowledge

► Hand out the **"Tone and Inflection" Warm-Up,** and have volunteers read the script aloud expressively.

► Ask, "How did the volunteers show the characters' feelings?" Explain that an actor's tone and inflection can show mood or emotions.

Teach

Time: About 15 minutes

Prepare Divide students into groups of four.

Lead

► Remind students that projection and enunciation are the safe use of volume and clarity to enable one's voice to be heard by an audience. Have them practice this by making the sound "ha" using their diaphragms while projecting it progressively farther away.

► Have each group assign the roles of the **Warm-Up** characters. Groups with more or less than four may combine characters or add new characters. Give students time to briefly plan an improvisation in which they will solve the problem presented in the **Warm-Up.**

► Have each group improvise while focusing on tone.

Informal Assessment Did each student participate in the improvisation and attempt to use vocal tone and inflection?

History and Culture

Tell students that playwrights use both words and silence to communicate meaning. The plays of Harold Pinter, for example, contain many meaningful silences, which are nicknamed "Pinter pauses." In these scenes, performers "fill the silence" in ways that communicate subtext. Have students repeat one of the improvisations, using extended pauses to communicate feelings and intentions.

Reflect

Time: About 5 minutes

► Discuss ways students projected characters' ideas and emotions.

Apply

 Journal: Observing
Have students describe in their journals observations they have made of the ways people speak to their pets.

Name _____   Date _____

Tone and Inflection

Read the conversation below in which four friends are discussing a problem they want to solve. Each character could be a boy or a girl. Imagine how the characters would sound if you were overhearing this conversation.

JORDAN: So when is the concert?

CHRIS: How many times do I have to tell you? Next Thursday!

CAMERON: What difference does it make—we're not going.

LEE: Don't be such a pessimist. There's always a chance . . .

CAMERON: Yeah—fat chance!

JORDAN: Wait a minute, wait a minute. Maybe we can figure something out.

CAMERON: Forget it! It's not going to happen. It's a school night, we don't have the money, and we need a ride. Three strikes and we're out.

CHRIS: All right, all right. Thanks for stating the problem. Now, let's think about a solution. There has to be a way.

LEE: You're right, and we're going to sit right here until we find it.

Objectives

🔍 Perception To review drama concepts about sound and voice and think about applications they have to real life

🎨 Creative Expression To plan and perform an improvisation using voice, music, and sound effects

〽 History and Culture To learn about the Beijing Opera

💬 Evaluation To thoughtfully and honestly evaluate one's own participation using the four steps of criticism

Materials

📄 Copies of "The Nightingale," pp. 132-134

○ Items with which to make sound effects, such as bells, alarm clocks, rattles, musical instruments, paper, paper clips; large books, cellophane, or small combs

○ Tape recorder (for recording and playing sound effects)

○ Tape or CD player (for playing music) and several recordings of traditional Chinese music

📄 Copies of the **Unit 4 Self-Criticism Questions**, p. 86

📄 Copies of the **Unit 4 Quick Quiz**, p. 87

○ *Artsource®* Performing Arts Resource Package (optional)

Standards

National Theatre Standard: The student researches by using cultural and historical information to support improvised and scripted scenes. The student applies research from print and nonprint sources to script writing, acting, design, and directing choices.

Lesson 6 Unit Activity: Improvisation

Focus

Time: About 10 minutes

Review Unit Concepts

"The dramatic elements of sound and voice are an important part of theatrical productions. Sound effects and music are useful for suggesting environment and mood. The human voice can be used to create character voices that communicate personality; variations in tone and inflection can express many different emotions." "Los elementos dramáticos de sonido y voz son una parte importante de las producciones dramáticas. Los efectos de sonido y la música son útiles para comunicar ambiente y taiante. Se puede usar la voz humana para crear voces de personajes que comunican personalidad; variaciones en tono e inflexión pueden expresar muchas emociones diferentes."

► Review with students the ways in which they explored the different aspects of sound and voice.

► Review the unit vocabulary on page 70.

〽 History and Culture

Have students research aspects of the Beijing Opera, the dominant theatrical form in China since the mid-nineteenth century, on the Internet. Plays in the Beijing Opera are based on text that is only an outline for the performance; the focus is upon conventions of acting, singing, and dancing. Music is very important in these plays, and traditionally the musicians sit upon the stage. If possible, have students find a clip of a Beijing Opera performance on the Internet or show a video that includes such a performance; compare and contrast elements of the performance with American dance, music, and theatre. Have students work to incorporate at least one element of the Beijing Opera into their improvisations of "The Nightingale."

Classroom Management Tips

The following are tips for managing your classroom during the **Rehearsals** and **Activity:**

✔ **Set Ground Rules** Tell students that whenever they hear a whistle, a bell, or some other distinctive sound of your choice, they must stop whatever they are doing.

✔ **Offer Support** During the **First** and **Second Rehearsals** make sure that each group has selected a note taker and group leader. These decisions will help provide structure to the activity. Reinforce the role of the group leader as a person who makes sure that everyone is included in all decision-making.

✔ **Encourage Creativity** During the **Second Rehearsal** be on the lookout for creative additions or adjustments that students bring to their development of character voices and sound effects.

Teach

First Rehearsal

▶ Distribute copies of **"The Nightingale"** on pages 132 through 134. Read the story aloud while students pantomime it in unison.

▶ Divide the class into four groups. Have each group select a note taker and a group leader. Assign each group one of the following:

(1) The scene in which the jeweled bird stopped singing.

(2) A conversation between the nightingale and jeweled bird.

(3) Officials discovering that the nightingale has left the palace.

(4) The emperor's courtiers returning and finding him well.

▶ Explain that each group should plan to use music and record sound effects for an improvisation of their scene; a tape recorder, tape or CD player, recordings of Chinese music, and items for creating sound effects will be available at the **Second Rehearsal.** They may also bring in sound effects items. *(See page T14 for more about Sound Effects.)*

▶ Have each group divide roles and make plans regarding their sound effects.

Second Rehearsal

▶ Have students get into their groups and locate their notes.

▶ Have groups take turns using sound effect objects to record their sound effects in the proper order and using the tape or CD player to listen to and select pieces of traditional Chinese music.

▶ Whenever groups are not working on sound effects or music, they should work on their improvisations. Group members should establish the ways they are going to speak and move, as well as which members might be available offstage at certain moments to cue and play the music or sound effects. Encourage them to use emotional and sense memory techniques from **Unit 2** when working on their characters.

▶ Give each group one turn using both their sound effects and music with their improvisation.

Sound and Voice Activity

▶ Have students create a space in the classroom for the improvisations. Allow students to create a simple setting. Set up the tape player and tape or CD player.

▶ Tell students that their goal is to improvise their scenes using vocal inflection, sound effects, and music. Remind them of safe voice use, including projection. Have each group set up for and perform its improvisation.

▶ Have students analyze their improvisations and audience behavior.

Standards

National Theatre Standard: The student analyzes improvised and scripted scenes for technical requirements. The student writes scripts by the creation of improvisations and scripted scenes based on personal experience and heritage, imagination, literature, and history.

Unit Links

Visual Arts: Balance

Visual artists, actors, and dancers all strive for balance in their art. Tell students that the visual artist plans an artwork using the type of balance that will best enhance his or her vision for the subject and the media. The actor and dancer seek an inner balance between the total absorption of portraying a character or the emotion of a dance and a constant awareness of the skills and techniques necessary to fully communicate that character or emotion to an audience. Have students discuss their own experience of seeking this balance in the **Sound and Voice Activity.**

Theatrical Arts Connection

Television Have students analyze a television program for the different sound effects used. If possible, tape a program of your choice and view it as a class. Have students take notes during their viewing. Discuss the sound effects they identified and discuss how they were probably achieved. Have students make suggestions as to how some of the same sounds might be recreated in the classroom.

Film/Video Acquire from a local library or video store a film version of "The Nightingale" that you can share with the class (such as that created by Shelley Duvall's *Fairytale Theatre*). After students view it, lead a discussion comparing and contrasting scenes from the film with their own improvisations.

Standards

National Theatre Standard: The student uses articulated criteria to describe, analyze, and constructively evaluate the perceived effectiveness of artistic choices found in dramatic performances.

Reflect

Time: About 10 minutes

Assessment

▶ Have students evaluate their participation by completing the **Unit 4 Self-Criticism Questions** on page 86.

▶ Use the assessment rubric to evaluate the students' participation in the **Unit Activity** and to assess their understanding of sound and voice.

▶ Have students complete the **Unit 4 Quick Quiz** on page 87.

	3 Points	2 Points	1 Point
Perception	Gives full attention to review of unit concepts and vocabulary words. Has mastered a connection between music, theme, and propaganda.	Gives partial attention to review of unit concepts and vocabulary words. Is developing an understanding of a connection between music, theme, and propaganda.	Gives little attention to review of unit concepts and vocabulary words. Has a minimal understanding of a connection between music, theme, and propaganda.
Creative Expression	Fully participates in the creation of sound effects, selection of music, creation of character voices, and all other aspects of the improvisation.	Fully participates in at least two of the following: creation of sound effects, selection of music, or creation of character voices.	Adequately participates in only one of the following: creation of sound effects, selection of music, or creation of character voices.
History and Culture	Fully participates in researching the Beijing Opera; clearly uses one aspect of this research in the improvisation.	Somewhat participates in researching the Beijing Opera; adequately uses one aspect of this research in the improvisation.	Shows poor participation in researching the Beijing Opera; does not clearly help his or her group to use one aspect of this research.
Evaluation	Thoughtfully and honestly evaluates own participation using the four steps of art criticism.	Attempts to evaluate own participation, but shows an incomplete understanding of evaluation criteria.	The students makes a poor attempt to evaluate own participation.

Apply

▶ Ask students, "What do you think is the theme, or main idea, that the writer of 'The Nightingale' wanted to communicate through the story? What is the story's meaning?" *(you do not appreciate something until it is gone; the meaning of true friendship)* Discuss real-life applications of these ideas.

▶ Discuss with students the effect music can have on an audience's mood. How could music be used to manipulate an audience or to convince them of propoganda? Discuss the ways in which theatre can be used to further social agendas, both good and bad.

View a Performance

ARTSOURCE

Sound and Voice in Dance

▶ Have students analyze elements of appropriate audience behavior when viewing a performance, including respectful silence and attention. Have them agree to apply this behavior during the performance.

▶ If you have the *Artsource*® videocassette or DVD, have students view "Isicathulo (Gum Boot Dance)" performed by the African American Dance Ensemble in South Africa.

▶ Have students discuss and write answers to the following questions:

Describe What types of sounds did you hear during the performance? *(jingling bells on the dancer's boots, clapping, slapping)* Describe the music. *(several drumbeats)* How did the performers use their voices? *(They called out and chanted.)*

Analyze How did the music create a particular mood? *(It made the dance seem exciting and energetic.)* How was the dance affected by the music? *(The music set the pace of their movements.)* Describe the dancers' characters. *(One dancer seemed to not know how to dance, so the others taught it to her.)*

Interpret Compare the work of these dancers with the work of other dancers you have seen in movies, music videos, or in live performances. What types of characters does each dancer portray?

Decide If you could add one sound effect to the performance, what would you add? What parts of the performance did you enjoy most?

```
"When a performance is over, what
remains? . . . It is the play's
central image that remains, its
silhouette, and if the elements are
rightly blended this silhouette will
be its meaning, this shape will be the
essence of what it has to say."

                        —Peter Brook,
             (1925-  ), director
```

LEARN ABOUT CAREERS IN THEATRE

Tell students that a theatre may have a permanent staff of individuals who make rehearsals run smoothly. A casting director assists in arranging casting sessions. A dramaturge, or literary manager, works with the director to select and prepare scripts for performance. He or she also provides information for the director and the actors about the history of the play and the various interpretations of the work. A voice and dialect coach works with actors on diction, breath control, and other technical aspects of projecting the voice. Some theatre groups have permanent people in these roles; others may hire them for a short period of time. Have students compare and contrast these careers; have interested students investigate the skills and training that are required for each of these careers in theatre and report them to the class.

Standards

National Theatre Standard: The student explains the knowledge, skills, and discipline needed to pursue careers and vocational opportunities in theatre, film, television, and electronic media.

Name _____ Date _____

Unit 4) Self-Criticism Questions

Think about how you contributed to the improvisation.
Then answer the questions below, selecting the part of
each question that applies to you.

1. **Describe** How did you use your voice when you were improvising your
character? How did you help select the music and record the sound effects?

_____

_____

_____

2. **Analyze** How did your voice express the character's thoughts and
emotions? How did the music you helped select and the sound effects
you helped to create show the mood or setting of the improvisation?

_____

_____

_____

3. **Interpret** Compare and contrast ideas shown through the music you
selected and music you often listen to. Which were the most effective
sound effects in the improvisation? Why?

_____

_____

_____

4. **Decide** If you could do this activity again, would you change anything
you did? Why or why not?

_____

_____

Name _____ Date _____

Unit 4 Quick Quiz

Completely fill in the bubble of the best answer for each question below.

1. **Sound effects are**
   - Ⓐ produced both live and as recordings.
   - Ⓑ the theme, or main idea, of a play.
   - Ⓒ only used in film.
   - Ⓓ always created by actors.

2. **Sound in theatre productions are usually used to**
   - Ⓕ bore the audience.
   - Ⓖ suggest a setting or environment.
   - Ⓗ take the place of costumes.
   - Ⓙ none of the above

3. **Voice in theatre productions is used to communicate**
   - Ⓐ the thoughts and emotions of characters.
   - Ⓑ meaning through movement.
   - Ⓒ only the setting of a play.
   - Ⓓ the audience's reaction to the play.

4. **Which sentence is *not* true?**
   - Ⓕ Music can cause an emotional response in the listener.
   - Ⓖ Characters do not usually have voices.
   - Ⓗ Tone and inflection are ways to communicate emotion.
   - Ⓙ Movement can be a response to music.

5. **Subtext is**
   - Ⓐ the meaning of a play.
   - Ⓑ a character's feelings not expressed through dialogue.
   - Ⓒ a character's feelings expressed through dialogue.
   - Ⓓ a type of script.

6. **Tone is**
   - Ⓕ the use of movement in a play, film, or television show.
   - Ⓖ only expressed through music.
   - Ⓗ a character's feelings not expressed through dialogue.
   - Ⓙ the use of pitch and volume to communicate an emotional message.

Score _____ (Top Score 6)

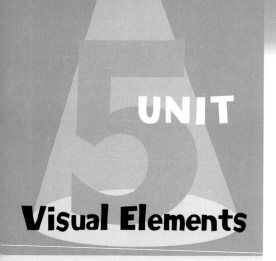

UNIT 5

Visual Elements

Unit Overview

Lesson 1 • Revealing Setting
Characters can reveal setting through pantomime. *Pantomime*

Lesson 2 • Costumes What an actor wears contributes to his or her characterization and to the setting of a play. *Costumes*

Lesson 3 • Makeup An actor's makeup has technical and aesthetic functions in a play. *Makeup*

Lesson 4 • Setting Scenery helps create the setting, or time and place, of a play. *Setting*

Lesson 5 • Props Floor, personal, and decorative properties are used to dress the stage and establish setting. *Props*

Lesson 6 • Unit Activity: Dramatized Literary Selection
This activity gives students the opportunity to use visual elements in a dramatization.

See pages T3–T20 for more about **Theatre Technique Tips.**

Introduce Unit Concepts

"An audience's response to a play depends on what they see as well as what they hear. Scenery, costumes, makeup, and props make visible the world of a play." *"La respuesta de un público a un drama depende tanto de lo que ve como de lo que oye. La escenografía, el vestuario, el maquillaje y los props hacen visible el mundo de un drama."*

Visual Elements

▶ Discuss how a person's clothes and the objects he or she uses can communicate information about him or her. *(A lab coat could show that a person is a medical professional, and so on.)*

▶ Discuss the types of information that can be learned by observing a setting. *(time of day or year, whether it is inside or outside, and so on)*

Vocabulary

Discuss the following vocabulary words.

floor properties propiedades del piso—also called floor props; objects found onstage

personal properties propiedades personales—also called personal props; objects used by actors onstage

decorative properties propiedades decorativas—also called decorative props; objects that establish setting but are not used by actors

stage crew equipo del escenario—backstage workers, including stagehands or grips who handle scenery and the prop crew, which handles properties

Unit Links

Visual Arts: Proportion, Distortion, and Scale

▶ Explain that proportion concerns the scale or size relationship of one part of an artwork to another; distortion occurs when normal proportions are altered. Discuss the effect of scenery that is disproportionately large. *(The actors would seem small.)*

▶ Show students a photograph of a portrait, such as *Frieda y Diego* by Frida Kahlo. Discuss the proportions of Frieda and Diego. *(She seems much smaller.)* Have students identify visual elements in the painting. *(a shawl, dress, paintbrush, and so on)*

Reading Theme: Ecology

▶ Ask students what they think of when they hear the word *ecology*. *(recycling, environment)* Discuss ecological problems that result from human activity. *(pollution, endangered species)*

▶ Have students identify their favorite natural settings, such as wildlife preserves, city parks, or the beach, and identify visual elements associated with them. *(grass, trees, and so on)*

Teacher Background

Background on Visual Elements

The visual elements of a play communicate concrete and abstract information to the audience. Costumes and makeup help the actors play their parts. Their colors and designs also work with the scenery to place the character in the setting and to show mood and theme. Props contribute to the setting, communicate information about characters, and help motivate a play's action.

Background on Technical Production

Visual elements are artistic and technical aspects of a dramatic production. When these elements align with the director's vision and interpretation of the play, they powerfully enhance the playwright's story and the actors' performances. However, when one or more of these elements are out of tune with the others, and most importantly, with the director's unifying vision, they become distractions to the audience and undermine the performance.

Research in Theatre Education

"In drama studies focused on such [interpersonal] relations, we see impacts on character understanding, comprehension of character motivation, increased peer-to-peer interactions, increased conflict-resolution skills, and improved problem-solving dispositions and strategies."

—James S. Catterall

"Essay: Research on Drama and Theatre in Education" in *Critical Links*

Differentiated Instruction

Reteach

Have students read a fable such as "The Fox and the Grapes" or "The Lion and the Mouse." Discuss their ideas for staging the fable. Keep track of their ideas for scenery, costumes, makeup, and props on the board.

Challenge

Have students select a time period and culture from their social studies curriculum, and have them design scenery, costumes, makeup, and props for a play that is set in that time and place.

Special Needs

Give all students an opportunity to fully experience each lesson activity. Some students with disabilities may excel in set, costume, or makeup design. Be sensitive to their abilities and preferences, giving them ample opportunities to perfect their newfound talents.

Theatre's Effects Across the Curriculum

★ **Reading/Writing**
   Reading Response Analyzing a story for the purpose of dramatization is another way to practice interpreting a written text.

★ **Math**
   Scale When students design scenery and props, they must consider the scale of such designs.

★ **Science**
   Predicting When students design costumes for a scene set in the future, they use information about the advantages and disadvantages of known materials to make predictions about how clothing could be altered and improved in the future.

★ **Social Studies**
   Culture Students become aware of the relationship between a society and its performing arts.

★ **Music**
   Volume When music is used in theatre, students acting as tech crew learn to balance volume between voices and music so that one does not overpower the other.

★ **Dance**
   Technical Aspects As students create scenery, they can identify a dancer's need for sturdy scenery that will allow him or her to safely move on, around, or through a set.

To consider how a setting can be established without the use of props

🎬 **Creative Expression**
To create a setting using pantomime

🏺 **History and Culture**
To learn about the Japanese tradition of Kabuki theatre

❗ **Evaluation** To informally evaluate one's own work

Materials

📄 Copies of **"Revealing Setting" Warm-Up,** p. 91

⭕ Journals or writing paper

Unit Links

Visual Arts: Scale
Scale is important in art and scene design. Tell students that scale is the proportion between two sets of dimensions, as in a drawing of a lamp and the lamp itself. Explain that in a play with realistic visual elements, the scale of the scenery should match the scale of the props; for example, a park bench and scenery depicting the trees in the park should share realistic proportions.

Standards

National Theatre Standard: The student, in an ensemble, interacts as an invented character.

Listening/Speaking Standard: The student demonstrates nonverbal cues to convey a message to an audience (for example, movement, gestures, facial expressions).

Reading Standard: The student is expected to interpret text ideas through such varied means as journal writing, discussion, enactment, and media.

Lesson 1 Revealing Setting

Focus

Time: About 10 minutes

"In this lesson we will use pantomime to show a setting." *(See page T3 for more about Pantomime.)*

Activate Prior Knowledge

▶ Hand out copies of **"Revealing Setting" Warm-Up,** and have students complete it. Have students pantomime the actions.

Teach

Time: About 15 minutes

Prepare Divide students into groups of four.

Lead Have students select one of the following environments for their pantomime: a beach scene, a grocery store, a crowded bus station, a construction site, or a restaurant. Remind them to consider the temperature, the weather, and any items in the setting.

▶ Give students time to establish a situation, characters, and a conflict.

▶ Have volunteers perform their pantomime, focusing on revealing the environment. Have the rest of the class guess the setting.

Informal Assessment Did each student participate in creating the pantomime?

🏺 History and Culture

Tell students that *Kabuki,* a traditional form of Japanese theatre, had its beginnings in the seventeenth century. These dance-dramas are performed to vocal and instrumental music. The costumes and makeup are extravagant. Most props onstage serve symbolic purposes; for example, the way an actor moves a fan can indicate opening a door or shooting a bow and arrow. Because of the skills to be mastered, a person wishing to become a Kabuki actor must begin training in childhood. The skills are passed down within families. Allow interested students to further investigate this form of theatre and report their findings. Have students replay their pantomimes using one prop symbolically.

Reflect

Time: About 5 minutes

▶ Discuss the challenges of showing setting through pantomime.

Apply

📓 Journal: Comparing
If possible, show students an online video of a talented actor performing a pantomime, such as Red Skelton playing his character "Freddy the Freeloader." Have students write a journal entry comparing this actor's work with the nonverbal communication of an actor of their choice.

Name _____ Date _____

Revealing Setting

Read the steps below. Imagine that you are an actor on an empty stage. How could you show this setting without props? Which actions would best show setting? Underline details of this setting that you could communicate without words.

1. It is a hot day. There is no air conditioning. You are sitting in a rocking chair in the kitchen of an old farmhouse.

2. A man comes into the room with a big metal pot of washed green beans. He tells you to break the green beans into smaller pieces. You do not want to do this.

3. You begin to break the beans in smaller pieces anyway.

4. After a few minutes you put the pot down.

5. You go to the cupboard and get a glass.

6. You open the refrigerator and pour lemonade into the glass.

7. You drink it down in one long drink.

8. Feeling better you go back to the rocker, put the pot back into your lap, and finish snapping the beans.

9. You take the pot to the sink, turn on the water, and add water to the beans. Then you take the pot to the stove and turn it on. You find a lid and put it on the pot.

10. You go back to relax in the rocking chair.

Objectives

 Perception To gather information to use in the design of a costume

 Creative Expression To select and design costumes for characters

 History and Culture To identify how film and television have depicted clothing of the future

Evaluation To informally evaluate one's own work

Materials

📄 Copies of **"Costumes" Warm-Up,** p. 93

○ Color pencils, crayons, or markers

○ Drawing paper

○ Construction paper, fabric, and other costume-creation materials

○ Journals or writing paper

Vocabulary

theme

Standards

National Theatre Standard: The student analyzes improvised and scripted scenes for technical requirements.

Listening/Speaking Standard: The student participates in classroom discussions using effective speaking strategies (for example, asking questions, making observations).

Science Standard: The student is expected to identify components of an ecosystem to which organisms may respond.

Lesson 2 **Costumes**

Focus

Time: About 10 minutes

"In this lesson we will select and design costumes for characters." *(See page T18 for more about Costumes.)*

Activate Prior Knowledge

▶ Hand out the **"Costumes" Warm-Up,** and have students complete it.

▶ Have students discuss their answers, using evidence from the script for support. Discuss the characters (they could be boys or girls), their actions, their environment, and the script's theme—the writer's attitude toward the subject.

Teach

Time: About 20 minutes

Prepare Divide students into pairs. Distribute costume materials.

Lead Say, "Each pair should design costumes for Mercurium or Razz. Each costume should help define the character, environment, his or her actions, and the script's theme."

▶ Encourage students to be creative; the clothing is from the future, so there is no right or wrong answer. They should include hats, shoes, and other accessories. Remind them to make their designs reflect their interpretation of characterization and theme.

▶ Have each student pair create one costume piece for each character's costume design, such as a hat or a wristband. Have them wear their costume pieces while performing the script.

Informal Assessment Did each student work cooperatively with a partner to design, create, and use costume pieces safely?

History and Culture

Discuss with students examples of futuristic clothing from television and film, such as clothing from *Star Trek* or *Star Wars*. These examples are notable for the wide variety of costuming required not only for the humans but also for the many alien life-forms present throughout the productions. Have student groups look for costume images from these shows or other science fiction films on the Internet, and compare and contrast them with their own costume designs.

Reflect

Time: About 5 minutes

▶ Discuss how different costumes helped define the characters, their actions, and their environment, as well as a theme.

Apply

Journal: Describing
Have students write journal entries describing one or more people they know whose clothing reflects their personalities.

Name _____ Date _____

Costumes

Read the conversation below. The characters are teenagers, and the setting is Earth 100 years from now. As you read, think about the personality of each character. On the lines below write two or three adjectives to describe each character's personality.

Mercurium: *(setting down a test tube and taking off her safety glasses)* This is frustrating. I've tried 30 different hybrids for my science experiment. Not one of them is still alive.

Razz: *(sitting down and slouching)* It's like I've been telling you. The air is way too poisonous out there for any plant to survive without an artificial atmosphere to protect it. Where do you think we'd be without the gear we wear when we go outside? Like dead, maybe?

Mercurium: Well, surely *something* can still live out there! I just have to find out what it is. That's what science is all about.

Razz: News flash! We already have that answer—the atmosphere is fatally toxic to living things and has been since 2070. We already know the answer to that question. Science is about answering questions that we *don't* have the answers to.

Mercurium: But suppose we could find something that can survive? *(Mercurium picks up her test tube and looks at it)* If we studied it, it might help us find a way to adjust other plants and animals so they could survive too.

Razz: *(getting up)* Here's a better idea: Figure out a way to get rid of the poison in the atmosphere. That way, living things can stay the way they are. We might actually be able to experience real sunshine, freshwater, and green stuff growing everywhere—you know, like all those pictures in the history books. If you're going to "devote your life to science," at least try to make Earth a better place in the process! *(Razz leaves the room)*

Adjectives that describe Mercurium:

_____

_____

Adjectives that describe Razz:

_____

_____

Objectives

 Perception To understand how makeup contributes to the portrayal of a character

 Creative Expression To design makeup to help establish a character

 History and Culture To learn about the use of masks in theatre

Evaluation To informally evaluate one's own work

Materials

- Copies of "Makeup" Warm-Up, p. 95
- Drawing paper
- Colored pencils, crayons, or markers
- Journals or writing paper

Unit Links

Visual Arts: Distortion

Distortion can be used to communicate. Explain that to make a character in theatre or a dance production less attractive, putty or makeup can be used to make one facial feature markedly out of proportion to others. Compare and contrast this use of distortion to communicate an idea and evoke emotions with the way distorted figures in artwork and distorted sounds in music might communicate.

Standards

National Theatre Standard: The student works collaboratively and safely to create elements of scenery, properties, lighting, and sound to signify environments, and costumes and makeup to suggest character.

Listening/Speaking Standard: The student participates in classroom discussions using effective speaking strategies (for example, asking questions, making observations).

Writing Standard: The student is expected to write to express, discover, record, develop, reflect on ideas, and to problem solve.

Lesson 3 Makeup

Focus

Time: About 10 minutes

"In this lesson we will create makeup designs to show different aspects of characters." *(See page T19 for more about Makeup and Masks.)*

Activate Prior Knowledge

► Discuss how makeup can contribute to character portrayal. *(It can change how an actor looks.)*

► Hand out the **"Makeup" Warm-Up,** and have students read it silently. Discuss the characters and their actions, relationships, and environment. Have volunteers read the script aloud, using their voices to create the characters.

Teach

Time: About 15 minutes

Prepare Divide students into groups of four, and distribute the materials for makeup design.

Lead Tell students to imagine they are makeup artists who are preparing to meet with the director to present ideas for each character. Their makeup should be practical and comfortable for the actors. It does not have to be realistic, but should at least suggest each animal from the **Warm-Up.** Everyone should work together, but each group member should draw the makeup plan for one animal.

► Have students share their ideas with the rest of the class. Discuss what they communicate about the characters and their actions, relationships, and environment.

Informal Assessment Did each student participate in the planning and produce one makeup design?

 History and Culture

Explain to students that masks would be another way to show the animals from the **Warm-Up.** Masks have been used since ancient times in drama and in ritual. Masks can be used with a costume that completely covers the wearer's body so the actor vanishes and the audience is invited to interact directly with the being or idea represented by the mask. If you wish, have students investigate the use of masks in a culture from their social studies curriculum. Students should prepare their reports orally or in writing and share them with the class.

Reflect

Time: About 5 minutes

► Compare and contrast students' different interpretations.

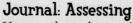 **Apply**

Journal: Assessing

Have each student write a journal entry assessing whether his or her makeup design communicated a theme of the **Warm-Up** and describing his or her personal reaction to this theme.

Makeup

The script below is an excerpt from a fictional meeting of the Animal Council's Executive Board of Windemere Woods, a mixed community of people and wildlife. The board is in emergency session to discuss the problem of humans.

The Dilemma

RABBIT: Something has to be done! Our food supplies are getting low. Some of the best green areas we have are being bulldozed. How big do humans' houses need to be, anyway? And what are we supposed to eat? You know how upset they get when we take an occasional meal from their yard or garden.

RACCOON: And then, of course, there are the traps and the poisons. What have we ever done to them?

SQUIRREL: I honestly don't see that we have any choice but to move on. The conditions here aren't going to get any better, and they'll probably get worse. We'd better get out while we still can.

DEER: Move on? On to where? It is all very well for you, Squirrel. As long as there is a tree somewhere, you can make a home. What about me? I need space to graze . . . to raise my family . . . to live. And even if I knew of such a place, just trying to get there could get me killed.

RACCOON: It's true. Deer's size and needs make it difficult to adapt. Temporary solutions that might work for some of us won't work for Deer. Some of my friends have decided to turn the tables on the humans. One family I know has taken up residence in the attic of one of those big houses. The humans never go up there, and it's a warm, dry place. Not the best situation, of course, but desperate times call for desperate measures!

Objectives

 Perception To consider how setting can be established

 Creative Expression
To create a setting using scenery

 History and Culture
To learn about theatrical resources available in the community

 Evaluation To informally evaluate one's own work

Materials

📋 Copies of **"Setting" Warm-Up,** p. 97

○ 1 large (at least 6' x 5') sheet of paper

○ 4 to 5 small (about 2' square) boxes, such as copier paper boxes

○ Tape, safety scissors

○ Orange, red, and brown construction paper

○ Brown and black poster paints and paintbrushes

○ Journals or writing paper

Vocabulary

stage crew

Standards

National Theatre Standard: The student, individually and in groups, creates characters, environments, and actions that create tension and suspense.

Listening/Speaking Standard: The student understands ways that culture and time influence a literary work.

Writing Standard: The student writes to express, discover, record, develop, reflect on ideas, and to problem solve.

Lesson 4 Setting

Focus
Time: About 10 minutes

"In this lesson we will create scenery for an improvisation." *(See page T17 for more about Settings.)*

Activate Prior Knowledge

▶ Hand out the **"Setting" Warm-Up.** Discuss the meanings of *renown, hew,* and *forbear.* Have students read the poem.

▶ Discuss how scenery could establish the poem's setting. Explain that although some scenery is realistic, symbolic scenery can be used to merely suggest a setting or to create a feeling.

Teach
Time: About 15 minutes

Prepare Divide students into two groups. Lay out scenery materials.

Lead Say, "The tree in the poem has lived for many years and might have been valuable to other people. We are going to safely create scenery for the tree and then improvise other stories near the tree."

▶ Have the first group use paint to decorate the large sheet of paper so it looks like bark. They will stack the boxes vertically and wrap this paper around them. Explain that the tree is so tall the trunk is all that will be seen onstage; in a real production, the top of the trunk might be masked with a curtain. Have the second group create leaves from the construction paper. These leaves can be scattered around the trunk.

▶ Have each group of students briefly decide on characters from history that might have interacted near this tree. Have them improvise these situations, incorporating props safely.

Informal Assessment Did each student create scenery safely and improvise a scene?

🏺 History and Culture

Most communities have several sources for theatrical productions nearby, such as schools, colleges, community theatre, or professional groups. Have students use the Internet or phone book to identify theatre in their area. If possible have the class attend such a production or tour a theatre and meet with its stage crew members.

Reflect
Time: About 5 minutes

▶ Discuss the pros and cons of realistic and symbolic scenery.

Apply

 Journal: Comparing
Have students write journal entries explaining the skills required to design sets for theatrical productions and comparing them with the skills required for another career.

Name _____ Date _____

Setting

Woodman, Spare That Tree!

by George Pope Morris

Woodman, spare that tree!
Touch not a single bough!
In youth it sheltered me,
And I'll protect it now.
'T was my forefather's hand
That placed it near his cot;
There, woodman, let it stand,
Thy axe shall harm it not.

That old familiar tree,
Whose glory and renown
Are spread o'er land and sea—
And wouldst thou hew it down?
Woodman, forbear thy stroke!
Cut not its earth-bound ties;
Oh, spare that aged oak
Now towering to the skies!

When but an idle boy,
I sought its grateful shade;
In all their gushing joy
Here, too, my sisters played.
My mother kissed me here;
My father pressed my hand—
Forgive this foolish tear,
But let that old oak stand.

My heart-strings round thee cling,
Close as thy bark, old friend!
Here shall the wild-bird sing,
And still thy branches bend.
Old tree! The storm still brave!
And, woodman, leave the spot;
While I've a hand to save,
Thy axe shall harm it not.

Props

Objectives

Perception To identify props to be used in a specific production

Creative Expression To select and use props in a dramatization

History and Culture To learn about the role of prop crews in theatrical productions

Evaluation To informally evaluate one's own work

Materials

📄 Copies of **"Props" Warm-Up,** p. 99

○ Possible prop items, including plates and dishes (paper or plastic), and other kitchen items

○ Journals or writing paper

Vocabulary

personal props
floor props
decorative props
prop crew
set
strike
spike

Standards

National Theatre Standard: The student works collaboratively and safely to create elements of scenery, properties, lighting, and sound to signify environments, and costumes and makeup to suggest character.

Listening/Speaking Standard: The student participates in classroom discussions using effective speaking strategies (for example, asking questions, making observations).

Reading Standard: The student is expected to understand literary terms such as *playwright, theatre, stage, act, dialogue, analogy,* and *scene* across a variety of literary forms.

Focus

Time: About 10 minutes

"In this lesson we will design and select props for a dramatization." *(See page T20 for more about Props.)*

Activate Prior Knowledge

▶ Hand out the **"Props" Warm-Up,** and have students read it. Discuss the story's characters and theme. *(The theme might be the importance of respect for elderly people, remembering that everyone will grow old one day.)*

▶ Discuss possible personal props, floor props, and decorative props for a dramatized version of this play.

Teach

Time: About 15 minutes

Prepare Divide students into groups of four. Set out props.

Lead

▶ Have groups examine the props you brought in and decide what other floor, decorative, and personal props might be useful in this story. Allow groups to create additional props using other objects in the classroom. They might also choose to use objects imaginatively.

▶ Have each group use their props while dramatizing the story.

Informal Assessment Did each student work to select props and dramatize the story using props safely?

 **History and Culture**

Explain to students that a prop crew, one part of the stage crew for productions, must make sure props are in their proper positions backstage and onstage before each performance. During scene changes prop crew members move, remove, and add props backstage and onstage. Have students choose one groups' setting from the dramatization. Have students practice setting (placing) and striking (removing) these props quickly. Discuss the benefits of spiking, or marking with small pieces of tape, the position of large props onstage and of planning who will move each prop in a scene change.

Reflect

Time: About 5 minutes

▶ Discuss how the students' use of props defined the action and environment. Did they also define characterization or theme?

Apply

📓 Journal: Explaining

Have students write a journal entry about the way people use certain objects or "props" to establish their identities and image, such as a key chain attached to a backpack.

Name _____ Date _____

Props

The Wooden Bowl

from *Grimm's Fairy Tales* by the Brothers Grimm (Adapted)

Once there was a young boy who lived with his parents and his grandfather. The boy loved his grandfather very much. They entertained each other for hours telling stories about far away places and adventures. Grandfather was quite old. He was not very steady on his feet, and his hands shook sometimes. The boy did not notice, but his mother was often annoyed with the old man. Although he tried very hard to be careful, sometimes he bumped into something or rattled a cup or plate. Every time this happened, she would scold him.

One day at dinner, Grandfather's hand shook so hard that he dropped a bowl, and it crashed to the floor and broke. The boy's mother was very angry and said that he could not eat from the good dishes anymore. She gave him an old cracked dish and a cup with no handle and told him he must eat his meals in the kitchen rather than in the dining room.

Grandfather's feelings were hurt, of course, but he said nothing. The boy was sad that his grandfather was no longer present during meals.

One afternoon a few days later, the boy's mother noticed that the boy was working busily on something. She came closer to see what was so absorbing. He had a small plank of wood and was carving out the center of it with his penknife. When his mother asked him what he was doing, he replied that he was making a bowl for her so she would have something to eat out of when she was older.

His mother looked into the eyes of her child. Her heart, which had been so full of impatience and anger, nearly broke as she realized how unkind and unfeeling she had been. She hugged her son, cried a few tears, and went into the kitchen to where Grandfather sat by the fireplace. Stooping down before him, she begged his forgiveness.

From then on, Grandfather took his meals with the rest of the family, and when something occasionally was broken, the pieces were just swept up and disposed of without any cross words.

Objectives

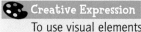 **Perception** To review concepts related to visual elements and to think about their applications in advertising

Creative Expression To use visual elements to dramatize a literary selection

History and Culture To apply research about the literature and art of India to visual elements appropriate for a dramatization

Evaluation To thoughtfully and honestly evaluate one's own participation using the four steps of criticism

Materials

- Copies of **"The Oldest of Trees,"** p. 135
- Drawing paper
- Colored pencils, crayons, or markers
- 1 large (at least 5' x 5') sheet of paper
- Face paint, mirrors, makeup remover, and cotton balls
- Copies of the **Unit 5 Self-Criticism Questions,** p. 104
- Copies of the **Unit 5 Quick Quiz,** p. 105
- *Artsource®* Performing Arts Resource Package (optional)

Standards

National Theatre Standard: The student explains how culture affects the content and production values of dramatic performances.

Lesson 6 Unit Activity: **Dramatized Literary Selection**

Focus
Time: About 10 minutes

Review Unit Concepts

"The visual elements of a play are effects that an audience can see during a production. Costumes, props, scenery, makeup, and lighting can help establish setting, define action and characters, and show a play's theme and mood." **"Los elementos visuales de un drama son todos esos efectos que un público puede ver durante una producción. El vestuario, los props, la escenografía, el maquillaje y la luz pueden ayudar a establecer el marco escénico, definir la acción y los personajes, y mostrar el tema y talante, o sentimiento, de un drama,"**

► Review with students the ways in which they explored visual elements in this unit.

► Review the unit vocabulary on page 88.

History and Culture

Tell students that many tales from India contain universal motifs such as punishment for dishonesty, assistance from magical objects, and reward for unselfishness. The last of these is a motif present in "The Oldest of Trees." Have students work in groups to investigate the culture, art, and clothing of India to aid them in the creations of visual elements for the dramatization. They can do their research on the Internet, using Web sites such as **www.hitchams.suffolk.sch.uk/india_art/index.htm** or **www.historyforkids.org.** (Choose *India* from the Geography section.) Have groups present informal reports on their findings, including at least three specific cultural details, and relate them to the dramatization.

Classroom Management Tips

The following are tips for managing your classroom during the **Rehearsals** and **Activity:**

✔ **Set Ground Rules** Have students agree on the ground rules for group participation before the **Activity** begins. After the **Activity,** have students evaluate their performance based on these ground rules.

✔ **Offer Support** During the **First Rehearsal,** make sure each group has selected a group leader. These decisions will help provide structure to the activity. Reinforce the role of the group leader as a person who makes sure everyone is included in decision making.

✔ **Provide Structure** During the **Second Rehearsal,** use your role as director to keep a tight focus on proceedings. You may wish to provide a fill-in-the-blanks outline for groups to use as they report on the visual elements they have developed.

Teach

Two 15-minute rehearsal periods
One 30-minute activity period

First Rehearsal

▶ Distribute copies of **"The Oldest of Trees"** on page 135. Read the story aloud as students follow along.

▶ Tell students that they are going to develop visual elements for a dramatization of this story. *(See page T17 for more about Settings.)* You will function as director. Discuss the story's theme—possibly "unselfishness is rewarded"—and its characters.

▶ Divide the class into four groups, distribute design materials, and assign the following tasks:

Group 1: Design a scenic backdrop. The scenery should use expressive design, or design that evokes theme and mood rather than seeming realistic. Such scenery might show a single image or stripe of color.

Group 2: Create costume designs for the king, tree, and woodsmen, including complete costumes (as for a professional production) and suggestions for simple costume elements, such as a crown for the king, for the dramatization. Take makeup designs into consideration.

Group 3: Create makeup designs for the king and the tree. Take costume designs into consideration.

Group 4: Create prop designs for the production, including recommendations for simple personal props.

▶ Have each group choose a "crew head" to chair the group.

Second Rehearsal

▶ Have students re-form their groups from the **First Rehearsal.** Have each group's "crew head" share the group's ideas and designs.

▶ Have the scenery group paint its scenic backdrop on the large sheet of paper. Have the prop group select or create personal props. Have the costume group select or create the simple costume elements. Have the makeup group experiment with face paint and their designs.

▶ Asking for volunteers, assign the roles of king, tree, and woodsmen, as well as townspeople, who also will be the stage crew.

Visual Elements Activity

▶ Have the class improvise the dramatization without visual elements. Emphasize that this performance will be in a presentational style. Have the townspeople form a chorus and stand in a semicircle around the center of the space. As director, coach students, taking suggestions from students when choices need to be made.

▶ Have the stage crew decide who will move props when. Have students hang the scenic backdrop; have actors put on their costumes and apply their makeup under the makeup designers' guidance.

▶ Have students perform their dramatization using all visual elements.

Standards

National Theatre Standard: The student works collaboratively and safely to create elements of scenery, properties, lighting, and sound to signify environments, and costumes and makeup to suggest character.

Unit Links

Visual Arts: Scale

Discuss the use of scale in artwork and designs for dance and theatre performances. Explain that in artwork with realistic scale, everything seems to fit together in relation to size; in artwork with unrealistic scale, the size relationships do not make sense. Designers of scenery for theatre and dance performances may also use realistic and unrealistic scales. Discuss stories that could be dramatized in dance or traditional theatre performances that might call for unrealistic scale to communicate a certain idea or evoke an emotion. *("Alice in Wonderland," "Jack and the Beanstalk," and so on)*

Theatrical Arts Connection

Television Show students a clip of an appropriate television program that depicts a time period other than the present, such as an episode of "Wishbone." Have students develop simple written observations of the program's technical details, including visual elements and sound.

Electronic Media Have students view an interactive CD-Rom and list its visual elements. Discuss the roles of different types of electronic media in American society. How do the visual elements in this CD-Rom help fulfill one such role? Have students research career opportunities in interactive Web and CD-Rom design.

Standards

National Theatre Standard: The student uses articulated criteria to describe, analyze, and constructively evaluate the perceived effectiveness of artistic choices found in dramatic performances.

Reflect

Time: About 10 minutes

Assessment

▶ Have students evaluate their participation by completing the **Unit 5 Self-Criticism Questions** on page 104.

▶ Use the assessment rubric to evaluate the students' participation in the **Unit Activity** and to assess their understanding of visual elements.

▶ Have students complete the **Unit 5 Quick Quiz** on page 105.

	3 Points	2 Points	1 Point
Perception	Gives full attention to review of unit concepts and vocabulary words, and masters an understanding of the importance of visual elements in real life.	Gives partial attention to review of unit concepts and vocabulary words, and is developing an understanding of the importance of visual elements in real life.	Gives minimal attention to review of unit concepts and vocabulary words, and has a minimal understanding of the importance of visual elements in real life.
Creative Expression	Fully contributes to both the creation of visual elements and dramatization of the story.	Fully contributes to one of the following: creation of visual elements or dramatization of the story.	Contributes minimally to the creation of visual elements and dramatization of the story.
History and Culture	Helps create an oral report that connects three findings from research to visual elements.	Helps create an oral report that connects two findings from research to visual elements.	Helps create an oral report that connects one finding from research to visual elements.
Evaluation	Thoughtfully and honestly evaluates own participation using the four steps of art criticism.	Attempts to evaluate own participation, but shows an incomplete understanding of evaluation criteria.	Makes a minimal attempt to evaluate own participation.

Apply

▶ Have students work together in groups to create television commercials based on the theme "Our natural environment is worth preserving." Allow them to create and select costume pieces, props, and scenic elements to help show each commercial's characters, action, setting, and theme. Have groups share their commercials with the class.

▶ Remind students that advertising is an important part of theatre; if plays are not promoted, people will not know about and attend them. Have students imagine they are going to promote their dramatization of "The Oldest of Trees." Discuss realistic visual elements they use to do this in their community. *(posters, flyers, and so on)* Have each student design a promotional poster for his or her dramatization.

View a Performance

Visual Elements in Dance

▶ Have students analyze the appropriate behavior that, as audience members, they should practice at every performance. Have students agree to apply this behavior.

▶ If you have the *Artsource*® videocassette or DVD, have students view "Sarve Kashmir," performed by the Djanbazian Dance Company. Alternatively, you may show them a video of another Persian dance performance. Explain that the "Sarve Kashmir" is a dance showing women selling bread on the streets of Zahedan, Iran.

▶ Have students discuss and write answers to the following questions:

Describe What visual elements do you see in this dance? *(shiny head scarves, gold jewelry, rust and blue costumes with gold decorations, a backdrop lit with violet light)* Describe the dancer's movements. *(turning hands, spinning, repetition, and so on)*

Analyze How do the visual elements add to the dance? *(They make it more interesting to watch; the scarves move with the dancers.)*

Interpret Compare the visual elements and music in this dance with the sights, movement, and sounds from the **Visual Elements Activity**, as well as sights, movement and sounds an audience would experience in a rock concert and in a sculptural art exhibit.

Decide What was your favorite visual element in this dance? Why?

LEARN ABOUT CAREERS IN THEATRE

Tell students that the role and function of the playwright in theatre cannot be overestimated. Playwrights provide the basis upon which many theatre productions rest. Explain that writing a play is not the same as writing a story. In some ways it is more difficult because many plays do not have descriptive passages to tell the audience about what someone is thinking or feeling. Everything in a play is communicated through movement, dialogue, and visual and technical effects. You may wish to have interested students attempt to write a script based on their dramatization of "The Oldest of Trees," including suggestions for staging and scenic design.

> "But the theatre is more than words:
> drama is a story that is lived and
> relived with each performance, and we
> can watch it live. The theatre appeals
> as much to the eye as to the ear."
>
> —Eugene Ionesco
> (1912–1994), playwright

Standards

National Theatre Standard: The student describes the characteristics and compares the presentation of characters, environments, and actions in theatre, musical theatre, dramatic media, dance, and visual arts.

Unit 5 Self-Criticism Questions

Think about how you contributed to the dramatization of "The Oldest of Trees." Then answer the questions below.

1. **Describe** What suggestions did you contribute for the visual elements your group created? Describe the scenery, props, costumes, or makeup you created.

   _____

   _____

   _____

2. **Analyze** How did the visual elements you created contribute to the characters, plot, or setting of the dramatization?

   _____

   _____

   _____

3. **Interpret** Compare the visual elements from your dramatization to what viewers see when they look at a painting, attend a ballet performance, and go to a musical concert.

   _____

   _____

   _____

4. **Decide** If you could do this activity again, would you change anything you did? Why or why not?

   _____

   _____

   _____

Name _____ Date _____

Unit 5 Quick Quiz

Completely fill in the bubble of the best answer for each question below.

1. Costumes are
- (A) a type of floor prop.
- (B) worn only by women onstage.
- (C) determined by the time and place of the play.
- (D) never important to characterization.

2. Scenery
- (F) suggests a setting or environment.
- (G) is an object used by actors.
- (H) is always made by actors.
- (J) provides the action of the play.

3. A stage crew member's job might include
- (A) acting onstage.
- (B) acting and directing.
- (C) directing and moving props backstage.
- (D) moving props backstage.

4. Personal props are
- (F) always created by the director.
- (G) changed after every performance.
- (H) objects used by actors onstage.
- (J) objects onstage that show time and place but are not used by actors.

5. The term *floor props* is defined as
- (A) "objects found onstage."
- (B) "objects onstage that show time and place but are not used by actors."
- (C) "objects held by actors onstage."
- (D) none of the above.

6. Makeup and masks do *not* show
- (F) a character's age.
- (G) a character's personality.
- (H) when and where a character lives.
- (J) a character's name.

Score _____ (Top Score 6)

UNIT 6

Subject, Theme, and Mood

Unit Overview

Lesson 1 • **Subject and Theme**
Theme is an attitude toward a play's subject; subject and theme are expressed through the action of a play. *Improvisation*

Lesson 2 • **Finding Mood** Mood is the emotional atmosphere of the play. *Creative Movement*

Lesson 3 • **Setting Creates Mood** Music, lighting, scenery, and sound effects can communicate mood nonverbally. *Pantomime*

Lesson 4 • **Characters Create Mood** Actors can help create mood through what they say and do as characters. *Tableau*

Lesson 5 • **Directors Show Theme** Directors unify a production through theme. *Improvisation*

Lesson 6 • **Unit Activity: Scripted Play** This activity will give students the opportunity to express subject, theme, and mood through script writing.

See pages T3–T20 for more about **Theatre Technique Tips.**

Introduce Unit Concepts

"Subject, theme, and mood form a basis for a play's production; they create its message and thought." *"El sujeto, el tema y el talante forman la base por la producción de un drama; crean su mensaje y sus ideas."*

Subject, Theme, and Mood

► Explain that the subject is what a play, television program, or film is about. Provide a subject, such as "family life," and brainstorm statements that reflect attitudes toward the subject. (Themes for "family life" could include "a family that is close can get through difficult times" or "having fun is an important part of family life.")

► Have students describe possible moods for each of the following plays: a mystery *(gloomy)* and a musical *(lighthearted)*.

Vocabulary

Discuss the following vocabulary words.

subject sujeto—one of a play's central ideas; answers the question "What is this play about?"

theme tema—an attitude toward a subject as expressed in a play

mood talante—the emotional atmosphere of a play

presentational theatre el teatro de presentación—an approach to theatre in which it is made obvious that the play is a play and not like real life

representational theatre el teatro de representación—an approach to theatre in which a production is designed to imitate real life

Unit Links

Visual Arts: Variety, Harmony, and Unity
► Explain that variety, harmony, and unity relate to the organization and use of elements, such as line and color, to communicate ideas in an artwork. Similarly elements of theatre, such as sound or visual elements, help communicate theme.

► Show the image of a painting, such as *Brooding Woman* by Paul Gauguin. Discuss how repeated and contrasting colors create harmony, variety, and unity.

Reading Theme: A Question of Value
► Have students brainstorm what they think of when they hear the word *value. (worth, money, expensive)*

► Discuss stories in which characters decide that certain things, such as friendship, are more important than money.

Teacher Background

Background on Subject, Theme, and Mood

Although a playwright may have a certain theme in mind when he or she writes a play, the director of a particular production must choose between possible subjects and themes, and use these to determine a production's mood, or emotional tone. Subject and theme in theatrical interpretation are used differently than in literary interpretation; subject here is more like theme in literature and refers to a central idea, while theme is the attitude toward a subject expressed through a play.

Background on Dramaturgy

While a director usually determines a production's subject and theme, a dramaturge is a consultant who helps the director make these decisions. A dramaturge helps evaluate plays and researches historical and literary questions that arise during rehearsals. A dramaturge might also gather information related to other productions of a play.

Research in Theatre Education

"Sustained student involvement in theatre arts . . . associates with a variety of developments for youth: gains in reading proficiency, gains in self concept and motivation, and higher levels of empathy and tolerance for others."

—James S. Catterall, Richard Chapleau, and John Iwanaga

"Involvement in the Arts and Human Development: General Involvement and Intensive Involvement in Music and Theatre Arts."

Differentiated Instruction

Reteach
Have students locate three pictures in magazines that suggest different subjects and themes. Below each picture have them state a subject in one or two words and a theme in the form of a sentence.

Challenge
Have students imagine that they are playwrights and select one subject that might interest them for a play. Have students develop three themes and determine the one they would use.

Special Needs
Some students with special needs may struggle with low self-esteem and thus remain passive during group activities. Encourage their participation by discussing and modeling group norms of acceptance and interdependence.

Theatre's Effects Across the Curriculum

★ **Reading/Writing**
Reading Response Analyzing a story for the purpose of expressing mood through creative movement is another way to practice interpreting a written text.

★ **Math**
Measurement When students design a setting to communicate a specific mood they must use math skills such as measurement and proportion.

★ **Science**
Observing When students construct an environment for drama they must use observations of environments to create the setting.

★ **Social Studies**
Culture When students interpret stories from other cultures they must consider other cultural points of view.

★ **Music**
Theme with Variations As students identify the ways different directors interpret productions in unique ways, they can better understand the way different musical arrangers can interpret the same melody using a wide variety of styles.

★ **Dance**
Problem Solving As students work to find many solutions to the same dramatic problems, they better understand the way in which dancers can express one theme in many ways.

Objectives

 Perception To identify subject and theme in a dramatization of a poem

 Creative Expression
To use improvisation to explore the theme of the poem

 History and Culture
To identify subject and theme in publicity materials

 Evaluation To informally evaluate one's own work

Materials

📄 Copies of "Subject and Theme" Warm-Up, p. 109

⭕ Journals or writing paper

Vocabulary

subject
theme

Standards

National Theatre Standard: The student describes and analyzes the effect of publicity, study guides, programs, and physical environments on audience response and appreciation of dramatic performances.

Listening/Speaking Standard: The student participates in classroom discussion using effective speaking strategies (for example, asking questions and making observations).

Visual Art Standard: The student illustrates themes from direct observation, personal experience, and traditional events.

Lesson 1 Subject and Theme

Focus

Time: About 10 minutes

"In this lesson we will use theme in an improvisation." *(See page T4 for more about Improvisation.)*

Activate Prior Knowledge

▶ Discuss the meanings of *treasury, purloin,* and *minting*. Distribute copies of the **"Subject and Theme" Warm-Up.** Read it aloud, and then have students do a choral reading of the poem.

▶ Discuss possible subjects for a dramatization of this poem. *(value, memory)* What attitude is expressed toward each subject? *(Beautiful memories are more valuable than money, and so on.)*

Teach

Time: About 15 minutes

Prepare Divide students into groups of four.

Lead Explain that all of the improvisations will illustrate a theme of the poem— "wonderful memories are more valuable than money" —in different ways. The theme can be communicated through what characters say and do; for example, a family could go camping instead of spending money at a theme park and end up having fun.

▶ Have each group choose a "director" to act as leader. Have the directors assign roles. Allow a few minutes for improvisation. The directors should give feedback as they work.

▶ If possible, have each student take a turn as director.

Informal Assessment Did each student participate in the improvisation?

 History and Culture

Promotional materials can help communicate a production's subject. Explain that different forms of publicity, such as flyers and radio spots, can arouse curiosity. Theatre programs may contain a synopsis of the play and background information gathered by a dramaturge, a production's expert on dramatic composition and theatrical representation. If possible, have students look online at posters promoting appropriate movies or plays, and have students guess the subjects or themes.

Reflect

Time: About 5 minutes

▶ Have students compare and contrast their improvisations.

 **Apply**

📓 **Journal: Designing**
Have students design in their journals a poster for a play based on the theme of "The Coin" that utilizes a special memory they have.

Name _____ Date _____

Subject and Theme

The Coin
by Sara Teasdale

Into my heart's treasury
I slipped a coin
That time cannot take
Nor a thief purloin—
Oh, better than the minting
Of a gold-crowned king
Is the safe-kept memory
Of a lovely thing.

Unit Links Reading: A Question of Value

Objectives

Perception To identify music that could show mood

Creative Expression To express mood using creative movement

History and Culture To learn about different styles of plays

Evaluation To informally evaluate one's own work

Materials

- Copies of **"Finding Mood" Warm-Up,** p. 111

- Tape or CD player and recordings of instrumental music that suggests several moods, such as tension, joy, and so on

- Journals or writing paper

Vocabulary

mood
comedy
tragedy

Standards

National Theatre Standard: The student incorporates examples of dance, music, and visual arts to express ideas and emotions in improvised and scripted scenes.

Listening/Speaking Standard: The student follows verbal directions.

Reading/Comprehension Standard: The student is expected to read classic and contemporary works.

Lesson 2 Finding Mood

Focus

Time: About 10 minutes

"In this lesson we will use creative movement to show mood." *(See page T12 for more about Creative Movement.)*

Activate Prior Knowledge

▶ Distribute the **"Finding Mood" Warm-Up,** have volunteers read sections of the story aloud, and have students divide the story into acts.

▶ Discuss why students chose to divide the story as they did. Suggest that part of their decisions had to do with the shifts in mood as the story progressed. Bring in music that reflects diverse moods, and have students assign music to each act.

Teach

Time: About 15 minutes

Prepare Have students stand.

Lead Tell students that they will move creatively at your direction to express the mood identified for each of the acts. Direct students through each of the following parts of the activity, saying, "begin" and "freeze" to begin and end each part:

▶ Move to suggest tension, greed, and unrest.

▶ Move to suggest frustration, grief, despair.

▶ Move to suggest gratitude and joy.

Informal Assessment Did each student use creative movement to interpret each of the three moods?

History and Culture

Explain that western theatre has traditionally divided plays into categories, including comedy and tragedy. These categories come from the ancient Greek theatre tradition. Traditionally, comedies are lighthearted and end happily, while tragedies end in a tragic or sorrowful way. Explain that, while these two broad categories are useful, they do not cover all modern dramatic experiences. Discuss other categories of plays, such as mysteries, parody, farce, satire, drama, and melodrama. Have students identify how the story of King Midas could be adapted to become a comedy or a tragedy.

Reflect

Time: About 5 minutes

▶ Discuss the ways students used movement to support mood.

Apply

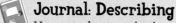

Journal: Describing
Have students write journal entries describing the types of music they like to listen to when they are in certain moods.

Finding Mood

Read the legend below. Imagine that the legend is a play with three acts. Circle and label the part of the story that you think should be in Act 1, Act 2, and Act 3.

King Midas and the Golden Touch

a Greek legend

There once was a king named Midas who was a good and fair man. He ruled his kingdom wisely, and he loved his family very much. However, Midas had one fault. Even though he had a great fortune, he had become very greedy.

One day it happened that Midas did a favor for the mighty Dionysus. In return, Dionysus granted Midas one wish. Midas told Dionysus that he wanted everything he touched to turn to gold. Dionysus warned him he might be sorry, but he gave him his wish just the same.

Midas soon saw that there would be problems with his new ability. On a walk through his gardens, he bent to smell a beautiful flower. As his nose touched the blossom, it turned from bright red to hard gold, and it no longer had any fragrance at all.

He returned to the palace and ordered a great feast to celebrate. His friends had a wonderful time feasting on all the delicious foods. Midas, however, could eat nothing. The instant his lips touched the food, it hardened into metal.

This went on for some weeks. The king grew thin and weak. His family, friends, and servants no longer went to see him. They were afraid that he would touch them accidentally and turn them into gold statues.

Then one day a terrible thing happened. His youngest daughter, who was too young to understand the danger, came running to her father. She had a flower to give him. Without thinking, Midas reached down and placed his hand on her hair. In horror, he drew back his hand as he saw that his beautiful child had been turned into a golden statue.

It was then that the Midas realized that he could bear this gift no longer. He went to Dionysus and begged to be released from the power of his wish. He wanted things as they had been before. Dionysus took pity on him and gave him his request.

The king was filled with joy. Everything that mattered was given back to him: his beloved child, good food, the beauty of nature, and his family and friends. Midas was still a rich man, but he never valued money in the same way. He had discovered that life is full of many treasures, and he appreciated them all.

Objectives

 Perception To understand ways that setting creates mood in dramatic productions

 Creative Expression To communicate the mood of a setting through pantomime

 History and Culture To learn about three types of theatre architecture

 Evaluation To informally evaluate one's own work

Materials

📄 Copies of "Setting Creates Mood" Warm-Up, p. 113

○ Journals or writing paper

Vocabulary

proscenium
arena
thrust

Standards

National Theatre Standard: The student explains the functions and interrelated nature of scenery, properties, lighting, sound, costumes, and makeup in creating an environment appropriate for the drama.

Listening/Speaking Standard: The student is expected to present dramatic interpretations of experiences, stories, poems, or plays to communicate.

Geography Standard: The student is expected to analyze the effects of physical processes and the physical environment on humans.

Lesson 3 Setting Creates Mood

Focus
Time: About 10 minutes

"In this lesson we will use pantomime to create a setting that shows mood." *(See page T3 for more about Pantomime.)*

Activate Prior Knowledge

▶ Hand out the **"Setting Creates Mood" Warm-Up.** Discuss the mood that the details communicate. Have students complete the **Warm-Up.**

▶ Discuss students' ideas, using the details as a standard to evaluate them. Discuss whether each drawing captures the appropriate mood.

Teach
Time: About 15 minutes

Prepare Divide students into groups of four.

Lead

▶ Explain that each group should pantomime the situation from the **Warm-Up,** communicating the setting and its mood as it affects each family member. Allow time to divide roles and plan, reminding them to use their ideas from the **Warm-Up** and to make individual character choices, since people may have many reactions to one situation.

▶ Have groups perform their pantomimes for the class.

Informal Assessment Did each student participate in the pantomime while working to communicate mood and setting?

 History and Culture

Tell students that in the history of western theatre there have been several types of theatre stages. The proscenium is a picture-frame stage; the audience sits in front of the stage and looks into the "frame." This frame hides all the stage machinery and lighting instruments. The thrust, or open stage, juts out into the audience, which is seated on three sides. The arena, or theatre-in-the-round, has a stage at the center of a square or circle. The audience surrounds the stage. Have students do an image search online to view examples of each type of stage. Discuss how students would need to alter their visual elements ideas in the **Warm-Up** to communicate mood on each of these stage types.

Reflect
Time: About 5 minutes

▶ Discuss how students communicated setting and created mood.

Apply

 **Journal: Describing**
Have students describe in their journals the way different physical environments affect their moods.

Name _____ Date _____

Setting Creates Mood

Read the details below. Design an environment to create a mood that would match these details. Write your ideas for scenery, props, lighting, and sound effects on the lines below, and then draw the environment in the box below.

> **Time:** present day; late at night
>
> **Weather Conditions:** howling storm of wind and rain
>
> **Place:** deserted farmhouse
>
> **Situation:** A family is stranded when their car breaks down; their cell phone cannot get a signal in this area.

Scenery _____

Props _____

Lighting _____

Sound Effects _____

Objectives

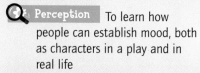 **Perception** To learn how people can establish mood, both as characters in a play and in real life

Creative Expression To create mood using tableau

History and Culture To learn about presentational and representational styles of theatre production

Evaluation To informally evaluate one's own work

Materials

- Journals or writing paper

Vocabulary

presentational theatre
representational theatre

Unit Links

Visual Arts: Variety
Have students compare and describe examples of aural, oral, visual, and kinetic variety in art, theatre, music, and dance. Explain that artists can use techniques such as contrast to communicate feelings. In theatre the playwright can create contrast through the conflict between the protagonist and an antagonist. Discuss the ways music in a play can emphasize contrasting character roles in the action.

Standards

National Theatre Standard: The student articulates and supports the meanings constructed from their and others' dramatic performances.

Listening/Speaking Standard: The student demonstrates nonverbal cues to convey a message to an audience (for example, movement, gestures, facial expressions).

Social Studies Standard: The student identifies different points of view about an issue or topic.

Lesson 4 Characters Create Mood

Focus

Time: About 10 minutes

"In this lesson we will use tableau to illustrate mood." *(See page T7 for more about Tableau.)*

Activate Prior Knowledge

▶ Read aloud **"The Apple Dumpling."**

▶ Ask students to describe the story's mood using examples from the story. *(cheerful, optimistic)* Compare each character's moods. Point out that, after contact with Mary, unhappy characters are content.

Teach

Time: About 15 minutes

Prepare Divide students into groups of four.

Lead Explain that each group will create two tableaux to illustrate the mood of two interactions in the story, such as Mary and the woman with the goose or Mary and the depressed man.

▶ Circulate as students plan their tableaux. Have groups present their tableaux. Discuss the meaning of each tableau, the moods that are apparent in the posture of each character, and how these moods relate to the overall mood of the scene.

Informal Assessment Did each student participate in the creation of two tableaux?

History and Culture

Explain that presentational theatre works toward a performance that is not realistic; it is clear that the actors, with the help of music, lighting, and costumes, are performing. Ancient Greek plays and many modern experimental plays are examples of presentational theatre. Representational theatre began in Europe in the mid-nineteenth century. In this style the audience should engage in "suspension of disbelief," or the ability to imagine that they are viewing real people. Playwrights who wrote plays for this production style were Henrik Ibsen and Anton Chekhov. Have students realistically dramatize the scenes from each tableau and then dramatize them as a musical theatre number to show the contrast between these styles.

Reflect

Time: About 5 minutes

▶ Have students discuss other ways they could have shown mood in their tableaux through music, lighting, or visual elements.

Apply

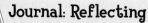 **Journal: Reflecting**
Have each student write a journal entry reflecting on how a person's positive or negative outlook affects his or her mood.

The Apple Dumpling

a folktale from England

There once was a woman named Mary who wanted an apple dumpling for supper, but although she had many plums, she did not have any apples.

"Someone in this world may have apples but wish for plums," she said to herself, and she went off with a basket of plums.

She came to a woman who was feeding some geese.

"Have you any apples for plums?" Mary asked.

"My husband loves plum jelly," the woman replied. "Would you take goose feathers instead of apples?"

"One pleased is better than two disappointed," Mary said, and she traded the plums for a bag of feathers.

Soon Mary came to a beautiful garden in which a man and woman were arguing.

"Cotton!" said the woman.

"Straw!" said the man.

"You there," cried the man, spotting Mary. "Which is better for stuffing a cushion: cotton or straw?"

"Neither," said Mary, smiling at them. "Feathers are best. For some apples I would trade this bag of feathers."

Having no apples, the man and woman offered her flowers, which Mary took, and she went on her way.

On the road Mary came to a young lord. His handsome face was wrinkled with frowns.

"Good day to you," Mary said, but the man only sighed.

"A good day I will not have," he said, "for I forgot the ring for my lady love, and so I have nothing to give."

"Take these flowers," said Mary, "and give them to your lady."

"Fair exchange is no robbery," said the lad, and he gave Mary his gold watch chain.

Mary thought happily, "I will sell this chain and buy apples!"

But no sooner had she reached the town then she saw a mother and children by a house, faces full of sadness.

"What is the matter?" Mary asked.

"Matter enough," said the mother, "when we have eaten our last crust of bread."

"Here," said Mary, giving them the gold chain. "Never will I eat an apple dumpling while neighbors lack bread."

The mother and children could not believe their eyes, and the mother cried out, "Thank you kindly! We do not have much to give, but here is our little dog."

Mary could not refuse, so she thanked them and led the puppy away.

Soon she passed a man on his porch with a sad look in his eyes. By the porch there stood a tree full of apples.

"A fine tree of apples!" Mary cried.

"Yes, but apples are no use," he said, "as I do not have so much as a dog for company."

In less time than it takes to tell it, Mary had given the dog to the man, asking "only a few of your apples in exchange."

"It only shows," Mary said, as she carried the apples home, "that if you try hard enough, you can always have an apple dumpling for supper!" And my, did she enjoy it!

Objectives

Perception To understand how directors generate plays' themes

Creative Expression To direct an improvisation that shows theme

History and Culture To compare and contrast the work of different directors

Evaluation To informally evaluate one's own work

Materials

- Copies of **"Directors Show Theme"** Warm-Up, p. 117

- Journals or writing paper

Standards

National Theatre Standard: The student describes and evaluates the effectiveness of students' contributions (as playwrights, actors, designers, and directors) in the collaborative process of developing improvised and scripted scenes.

Listening/Speaking Standard: The student demonstrates effective communication skills that reflect such demands as interviewing, reporting, requesting, and providing information.

Reading/Speaking Standard: The student is expected to offer observations, make connections, react, speculate, interpret, and raise questions in response to texts.

Lesson 5 Directors Show Theme

Focus

Time: About 10 minutes

"In this lesson we will direct an improvisation that shows theme."
(See page T4 for more about Improvisation.)

Activate Prior Knowledge

▶ Distribute the **"Directors Show Theme" Warm-Up,** and have students read the story.

▶ Explain that a director identifies the subject and theme on which a production will focus. Have students imagine they are directors of play versions of this story. Have them brainstorm possible subjects and themes and list them on the board. *(determination, value, inventiveness; a determined person will get what he or she wants, and so on.)*

Teach

Time: About 25 minutes

Prepare Divide students into groups of four.

Lead Assign each group one scene from the story, such as Ananse and his wife tricking Python or Ananse and his wife going to Sky-god.

▶ Have groups divide roles and select directors. Each group should choose one subject from the list and decide on the theme. Although they should all work together, the director will make the final decision about the theme and will make sure the improvisation shows this theme.

▶ Allow five minutes for discussion. After five minutes of improvisation, have new students act as directors. Repeat at five minute intervals until every student has had a turn acting as director. If you wish, allow volunteers to share their improvisation with the class.

Informal Assessment Did each student participate cooperatively as both an actor and a director?

History and Culture

Have student groups research the work of one of the following directors, focusing on themes of his or her productions: Billy Wilder, Ingmar Bergman, Elia Kazan, Alfred Hitchcock, or Mike Nichols. Have the class share their findings, comparing and contrasting each director's work.

Reflect

Time: About 5 minutes

▶ Have students evaluate their work as directors and how they influenced the way each improvisation showed theme.

Apply

Journal: Explaining

Have students write journal entries identifying a play or film that they would like to see remade with a focus on a different theme, explaining changes they would like to see.

Name _____   Date _____

Directors Show Theme

Ananse and the Stories

The tales about Ananse the Spider began centuries ago in Western Africa. The storytellers of the Ashanti people incorporated many traditional African values into these tales including verbal ability, wit, and strength. The following is one of the most famous Ananse tales.

It seems that Sky-god announced one day that he would be willing to sell the people's stories for the right price. Ananse, who spun beautiful webs, wanted to spin beautiful stories as well. Ananse, his wife, and his mother talked over the possibility of getting the stories. It was clear that Ananse valued the stories above everything, so his wife and mother agreed to help him get them.

The very next day, Ananse went to see Sky-god to learn the price for the stories. He was told that if he brought Python, Leopard, a swarm of bees, and the Jungle Sprite to Sky-god, he could have the stories. Sky-god did not think there was any chance that Ananse would succeed. However, Ananse and his wife were very clever.

Over the next few days, they made their plans. Ananse's wife had very good ideas and Ananse was very good at carrying them out. First, Python was tricked into getting tied to a pole. Ananse and his wife went to Python's house and argued about whether Python was longer or shorter than the pole. They asked him if he would settle the argument by allowing himself to be tied to the pole and then measured. Python agreed, and Ananse immediately took him to Sky-god.

Next, Leopard was tricked into getting into a sack. Ananse and his wife argued about whether Leopard would fit in the sack or not. As soon as Leopard was in the sack, they closed it up, and Ananse took him off to Sky-god.

To capture the bees, Ananse poured water into the hive and then invited the bees to hide in a pot until their hive was dry. As soon as they entered it, he slammed the lid on the pot and took it to Sky-god.

Finally, to capture the Jungle Sprite, Ananse and his wife prepared the Sprite's favorite food and placed it in the hands of a sticky gum doll. When the Sprite tried to take the food, he stuck fast to the gum figure and could not get loose. Then Ananse and his wife pushed the Sprite and the gum figure onto some palm leaves and took them to Sky-god.

The next day, Ananse went to get the stories. Sky-god was pleased with the imagination and wisdom that Ananse and his wife had shown. He gave the people's stories to Ananse. And that is how the Sky-god stories became called Ananse stories.

Objectives

 Perception To review the concepts of subject, theme, and mood and to learn how lines from plays speak to people's real lives

 Creative Expression To write a short script

 History and Culture To apply research to better understand and appreciate the life, work, and times of William Shakespeare

 Evaluation To thoughtfully and honestly evaluate one's own participation using the four steps of criticism

Materials

○ Lined writing paper

▤ Copies of the **Unit 6 Self-Criticism Questions,** p. 122

▤ Copies of the **Unit 6 Quick Quiz,** p. 123

○ *Artsource*® **Performing Arts Resource Package** (optional)

Standards

National Theatre Standard: The student describes and compares universal characters and situations in dramas from and about various cultures and historical periods, illustrates in improvised and scripted scenes, and discusses how theatre reflects a culture.

Unit Activity: Scripted Play

Focus

Time: About 10 minutes

Review Unit Concepts

"Subject, theme, and mood are determined by a director's interpretation and analysis of the text a playwright has written. The subject is what the play is about, such as 'justice' or 'revenge.' A play can have more than one subject. The theme is the attitude toward the subject expressed through the play's action. A play's mood is the emotional atmosphere of the play." "**El sujeto, el tema y el talante son determinados por la interpretación y análisis que el director hace del texto que un dramaturgo escribió. El sujeto es de que se trata un drama, como 'justicia' o 'venganza.' Un drama puede tener más de un sujeto. El tema es la actitud hacia el sujeto expresada a través de la acción del drama. El talante del drama es el ambiente emocional del drama.**"

► Review with students the ways in which they explored aspects of subject, theme, and mood in this unit.

► Review the unit vocabulary on page 106.

History and Culture

Tell students that William Shakespeare, who lived from 1564 to 1616, is considered one of the greatest English playwrights of all time. His plays, which are generally divided into comedies, tragedies, and history plays, are still performed all over the world. They are valued for their inventive plots, universal themes, and characters, and their poetic use of language. Not much is known about Shakespeare's life. He lived in England, received a solid education at a local school, and then joined a traveling theatre group as an actor. Soon after, he began writing plays. In 1599, he became part owner of the Globe Theatre, a popular theatre in London. Shakespeare's words have endured for 400 years and still have the power to reach and deeply move audiences of today. After students write their scripts, have them compare and contrast one character they each created with three of the characters from *King Lear*.

Classroom Management Tips

The following are tips for managing your classroom during the **Rehearsals** and **Activity:**

✔ **Set Ground Rules** Tell students that a collaborative process such as script writing requires everyone in the group to focus on the task.

✔ **Offer Support** For students who seem to be "stuck," have them improvise situations from their own lives that relate to the subject and use these improvisations to help them consider the theme.

✔ **Encourage Creativity** Encourage students to make revisions based on hearing the tone of voice and delivery of the actors. Remind students that a script is meant to be heard, not read silently.

Teach

First Rehearsal

▶ List the following characters on the board: King Lear, Goneril, Regan, Cordelia, the Earl of Kent, the Duke of Burgundy, the King of France, the Fool, the Duke of Albany, and Edmund. Have students copy this list on writing paper and take notes about each character as you read.

▶ Read aloud **"King Lear"** on pages 136 through 138, making sure to dramatize each character when speaking the lines. Pause throughout the reading, allowing students to summarize the plot's events and to ask questions. Have students identify the characters, their relationships, and their environment.

▶ Tell students that this version is shortened and adapted from Shakespeare's play, but that the character's speech was written four hundred years ago. If possible show an annotated page from the play and discuss the older form of English used.

▶ Discuss students' ideas about subject, theme, and mood, and have students list them on their paper. Suggest that some possible subjects and themes, such as "family conflict" or "greed destroys," are universal and transcend time and place.

Second Rehearsal

▶ Divide students into groups of three. Explain that each group will create a short scripted scene that reflects one of the subject and themes suggested by *King Lear. (See page T10 for more about Script Writing.)*

▶ Have each group choose one student to record their ideas and then decide together on the subject and theme. Have them identify a real-life situation that would show this theme, making a list of characters and their traits. Then have them improvise their ideas and write a draft of the script. You might want to show them "Dr. Stockmann Takes a Stand" on pages 128–131 as a formatting model.

▶ You may wish to allow students to work on this script during other class times after this **Rehearsal** and before the **Activity.** Review their drafts and give students feedback.

Subject, Theme, and Mood Activity

▶ Have students re-form groups from the **Second Rehearsal.** Pair groups, and explain that the groups in each pair will read each others' scripts out loud. Group members may read for more than one character if needed. After the first readings, students should discuss their scripts and make revisions.

▶ Before the end of the **Activity,** ask for volunteers to read one script for the class. Discuss the subject and theme of the script. If times allows, have each group perform their script as Reader's Theatre for the class. Discuss the collaborative artistic process.

Standards

National Theatre Standard: The student, individually and in groups, creates characters, environments, and actions that create tension and suspense. The student refines and records dialogue and action.

Visual Arts: Variety

Variety is essential to artwork, plays, and choreography. Tell students that variety in art is the principle of design concerned with difference or contrast; artists use elements such as line, color, and shape to create variety in artwork. Playwrights create variety by creating characters who contrast with each other, thus creating conflict and interesting character development. Discuss the way a choreographer could use variety in pace to create interest in a dance. *(The dancers could move fast and then slow, and so on.)*

Theatrical Arts Connection

Electronic Media Have students select three computer or video games that create different moods. Students should identify the mood of scenes from each game and provide examples from the action, visual elements, and music as evidence. Discuss the role of electronic media as entertainment. How does each mood relate to this function? *(A scary scene keeps a player interested and focused, and so on.)*

Film/Video Lead a discussion regarding popular themes that are present in films with which students are familiar. Ask students to brainstorm films that have one or more of the following themes: (1) Crime doesn't pay; (2) There is nothing more important than family; (3) Friendship is a precious gift; and (4) Growing up is a difficult task.

Standards

National Theatre Standard: The student uses articulated criteria to describe, analyze, and constructively evaluate the perceived effectiveness of artistic choices found in dramatic performances.

Reflect

Time: About 10 minutes

Assessment

▶ Have students evaluate their participation by completing the **Unit 6 Self-Criticism Questions** on page 122.

▶ Use the assessment rubric to evaluate the students' participation in the **Unit Activity** and to assess their understanding of subject, theme, and mood.

▶ Have students complete the **Unit 6 Quick Quiz** on page 123.

	3 Points	2 Points	1 Point
Perception	Gives full attention to review of unit concepts and vocabulary words. Masters an understanding of the connection between theme, a line from Shakespeare, and events in real life.	Gives partial attention to review of unit concepts and vocabulary words. Is developing an understanding of the connection between theme, a line from Shakespeare, and events in real life.	Gives minimal attention to review of unit concepts and vocabulary words. Has a minimal understanding of the connection between theme, a line from Shakespeare, and events in real life.
Creative Expression	Fully participates in all of the following: brainstorming script ideas, creating a rough draft, performing readings, and revising the script.	Participates in three of the following: brainstorming script ideas, creating a rough draft, performing readings, and revising the script.	Participates in one or two of the following: brainstorming script ideas, creating a rough draft, performing readings, and revising the script.
History and Culture	Clearly uses details from research while comparing and contrasting a character from his or her script with three characters from *King Lear.*	Clearly uses details from research while comparing and contrasting a character from his or her script with two characters from *King Lear.*	Clearly uses details from research while comparing and contrasting a character from his or her script with one character from *King Lear.*
Evaluation	Thoughtfully and honestly evaluates own participation using the four steps of art criticism.	Attempts to evaluate own participation, but shows an incomplete understanding of evaluation criteria.	Makes a minimal attempt to evaluate own participation.

Apply

▶ Write the following on the board: "What's in a name? That which we call a rose/ By any other word would smell as sweet." Explain that this quote is from another of Shakespeare's plays, *Romeo and Juliet.* Discuss what this phrase means. *(A person is not defined by a name or other external agents, but by who he or she really is.)* Explain that in the play Romeo and Juliet fall in love, but their families are fighting and so they cannot be together. Juliet says this after she finds out who Romeo's family is. This line summarizes the central struggle of the play.

▶ Explain that many phrases from Shakespeare's plays have become famous and known by people who may never have read the plays. Have students discuss examples from real life that prove or disprove the theme of the phrase from *Romeo and Juliet.*

View a Performance

Subject, Theme, and Mood in Animation Storyboards

▶ Have students identify elements of appropriate audience behavior when viewing a performance, including respectful silence and attention. Have them agree to apply this behavior during the performance.

▶ If you have the **Artsource**® audiocassette and videocassette or DVD, have students listen to the audio first and then watch the video for *Every Picture Tells a Story,* with music composed by Paul Tracey and storyboards created by John Ramirez. Alternatively, show part of an animated feature film.

▶ Have students discuss and write answers to the following questions:

Describe What sounds and instruments did you hear in each musical piece on the audio? *(cries of gulls, horn, rattle, flute, and so on)* What was the story told by the final storyboard? *(A man drives a "taxi cart," but gets greedy and puts too many people on the cart; and so on.)*

Analyze What moods were created by each piece of music? *(wistful, happy, peaceful but full of potential action)* How did the music create mood during the documentary and the final storyboard? *(One musical piece made the documentary and the filmed storyboard feel upbeat and silly, and so on.)* What are a possible subject and theme of the story? *(Greed; greed will lead to trouble in the end.)*

Interpret What scenes from your script would you include on a storyboard? What music would you use to accompany it? Compare and contrast the way play scripts, artwork on storyboards, and music can communicate oral, aural, visual, and kinetic elements.

Decide What did you learn about animation?

"Drama connects us with the past and makes it available, while affirming human values which transcend the concepts of past and present."

—Cecily O'Neill
professor/authority
on educational drama

LEARN ABOUT
CAREERS IN THEATRE

Tell students that a producer is the person who assembles the artistic team and management staff to produce a play. This person also finds people who will invest in the production with the understanding that if the play is successful, they will get their investment back plus a profit. The producer of a play is usually not involved in the daily work of preparing a production, but he or she does have the authority to hire and fire artistic personnel. One of the most successful producers in the English-language theatre is Britain's Cameron Mackintosh, who produced the musicals *Cats* and *Phantom of the Opera,* among others. Joseph Papp is a noted producer in the United States. He founded the New York Shakespeare Festival with performances in Central Park. He has also produced Broadway hits as well. Have students investigate the skills and training required to become a producer and report their findings in written or oral form.

Standards

National Theatre Standard: The student explains the knowledge, skills, and discipline needed to pursue careers and vocational opportunities in theatre, film, television, and electronic media.

Name _____ Date _____

Unit 6 Self-Criticism Questions

Think about how you contributed to the script writing.
Then answer the questions below.

1. **Describe** What suggestions for theme selection, characterization, and script ideas did you contribute?

_____

_____

_____

2. **Analyze** How did the suggestions that you made enhance the script's subject, theme, and mood?

_____

_____

_____

3. **Interpret** Compare the way your script communicated emotion with the way music and dance you listen to, watch, or sing and perform in real life make you feel.

_____

_____

_____

4. **Decide** If you could revise this script again, would you change anything? Why or why not?

_____

_____

_____

Unit 6 Quick Quiz

Completely fill in the bubble of the best answer for each question below.

1. **In theatre, *subject* is defined as**
   - Ⓐ "what the play is about."
   - Ⓑ "what makes a play successful."
   - Ⓒ "the emotional atmosphere of a play."
   - Ⓓ "what the audience experiences as visual effects."

2. **In theatre, theme is**
   - Ⓕ a method used by actors to develop character.
   - Ⓖ nonverbal communication suggested by the playwright.
   - Ⓗ the coordination of artistic and technical aspects of a play.
   - Ⓙ the attitude toward a subject that is communicated through a play's action.

3. **Mood is**
   - Ⓐ the emotional atmosphere of a play.
   - Ⓑ defined as "what a play is about."
   - Ⓒ usually not noticed by the audience in a production.
   - Ⓓ unrelated to subject and theme.

4. **A presentational theatre performance would *not***
   - Ⓕ try to seem like real life.
   - Ⓖ have actors.
   - Ⓗ use visual elements.
   - Ⓙ have a subject and a theme.

5. **A representational theatre performance**
   - Ⓐ does not attempt to create mood.
   - Ⓑ does not attempt to represent or show real life.
   - Ⓒ attempts to represent or show real life.
   - Ⓓ does not have actors.

6. **Which of the following statements is *false*?**
   - Ⓕ A play may have more than one theme.
   - Ⓖ The director usually has control over the creative aspects of a production.
   - Ⓗ The playwright is responsible for interpreting and analyzing a play.
   - Ⓙ The meaning of a play is communicated both verbally and nonverbally.

Score _____ (Top Score 6)

Harvey's First Catch

from *Captains Courageous* by Rudyard Kipling (Adapted)

Activity Story

When Harvey Cheyne, the over indulged son of a millionaire, falls overboard from an ocean liner, he is rescued by a Portuguese fisherman. Although at first he is angry and distant, he eventually joins the crew of We're Here, *a fishing boat, for a summer. In this excerpt Harvey deals with the challenges of fishing from a small boat, or rig, with the fisherman's son Dan.*

It was the forty-fathom slumber that clears the soul and eye and heart, and sends you to breakfast ravening. They emptied a big tin dish of juicy fragments of fish—the blood-ends the cook had collected overnight. They cleaned up the plates and pans of the elder mess, who were out fishing, sliced pork for the midday meal, swabbed down the fo'c'sle, filled the lamps, drew coal and water for the cook, and investigated the fore-hold, where the boat's stores were stacked. It was another perfect day—soft, mild, and clear; and Harvey breathed to the very bottom of his lungs.

"Dad," said Dan, "we've done our chores. Can't we go overside a piece? It's good catchin' weather."

"Not in that cherry-coloured rig near them ha'afbaked brown shoes. Give him somthin' fit to wear."

"Dad's pleased—that settles it," said Dan delightedly, dragging Harvey into the cabin. "Dad keeps my spare rig where he kin overhaul it, 'cause Ma sez I'm keerless." He rummaged through a locker, and in less than three minutes Harvey was adorned with fisherman's rubber boots that came half up his thigh, a heavy blue jersey well darned at the elbows, a pair of flippers, and a sou'wester.

"Now ye look somethin' like," said Dan. "Hurry!"

A little red dory, labeled Hattie S., lay astern of the schooner. Dan hauled in the painter and dropped lightly on to the bottom boards,

while Harvey tumbled clumsily after.

"That's no way o' gettin' into a boat," said Dan. "If there was any sea you'd go to the bottom, sure. You got to learn to meet her."

Dan fitted the thole-pins, took the forward thwart, and watched Harvey's work. The boy had rowed, in a ladylike fashion, on the Adirondack ponds; but there is a difference between squeaking pins and well-balanced rowlocks—light sculls and stubby, eight-foot sea-oars. They stuck in the gentle swell, and Harvey grunted.

"Short! Row short!" said Dan. "If you cramp your oar in any kind o' sea you're liable to turn her over. Ain't she a daisy? She's mine too."

The little dory was specklessly clean. In her bows lay a tiny anchor, two jugs of water, and some seventy fathoms of thin, brown dory-roding. A tin dinner-horn rested in cleats just under Harvey's right hand, beside an ugly looking maul, a short gaff, and a shorter wooden stick. A couple of lines, with very heavy leads and double cod-hooks, all neatly coiled on square reels, were stuck in their place by the gunwale.

"Where's the sail and mast?" said Harvey, for his hands were beginning to blister.

Dan chuckled. "Ye don't sail fishin'-dories much. Ye pull; but ye needn't pull so hard. Don't you wish you owned her?"

"Well, I guess my father might give me one or two if I asked him," Harvey replied. He had

Unit Links   Reading: Perseverance

been too busy to think much of his family till then.

"That's so. I forgot your dad's a millionaire. You don't act millionare-y any, now. But a dory an' craft an' gear"—Dan spoke as though she were a whale-boat—"costs a heap. Think your dad'd give you one fer—fer a pet like?"

"Shouldn't wonder. It would be 'most the only thing I haven't stuck him for yet."

"Must be an expensive kinda kid to home. Don't slitheroo that way, Harve. Short's the trick, because no sea's ever dead still, an' the swells'll—"

Crack! The loom of the oar kicked Harvey under the chin and knocked him backward.

"That was what I was goin' to say. I had to learn, too, but I wasn't more than eight years old when I got my schoolin'."

Harvey regained his seat with aching jaws and a frown.

"No good gettin' mad at things, Dad says. It's our own fault if we can't handle 'em, he says. Let's try here."

Dan's line was out long before Harvey had mastered the mystery of baiting and heaving out the leads. The dory drifted along easily. It was not worthwhile to anchor till they were sure of good ground.

"Here we come!" Dan shouted, and a shower of spray rattled on Harvey's shoulders as a big cod flapped and kicked alongside. "Muckle, Harvey, muckle! Under your hand! Quick!"

Evidently "muckle" could not be the dinner-horn, so Harvey passed over the maul, and Dan scientifically stunned the fish before he pulled it inboard, and wrenched out the hook with the short wooden stick he called a *gob-stick*. Then Harvey felt a tug and pulled up zealously.

"Why, these are strawberries!" he shouted. "Look!"

The hook had fouled among a bunch of strawberries, red on one side and white on the other—perfect reproductions of the land fruit, except there were no leaves, and the stem was all pipy and slimy.

"Don't touch 'em! Slat 'em off. Don't—" The warning came too late. Harvey had picked them from the hook and was admiring them.

"Ouch!" he cried, for his fingers throbbed as though he had grasped many nettles.

"Now ye know what strawberry-bottom means," said Dan. "Nothin' 'cept fish should be touched with the naked fingers, Dad says. Slat 'em off ag'in' the gunnel, an' bait up, Harv'. Lookin' won't help any. It's all in the wages."

Harvey smiled at the thought of his ten and a half dollars a month, and wondered what his mother would say if she could see him hanging over the edge of a fishing-dory in mid-ocean. She suffered agonies whenever he went out on Saranac Lake; and, by the way, Harvey remembered distinctly that he used to laugh at her anxieties. Suddenly the line flashed through his hand, stinging even through the "flippers," the woolen circlets supposed to protect it.

"He's a logy. Give him room accordin' to his strength," cried Dan. "I'll help ye."

"No, you won't," Harvey snapped, as he hung on to the line. "It's my first fish. Is—is it a whale?"

"Halibut, mebbe." Dan peered down into the water alongside, and flourished the big "muckle," ready for all chances. Something white and oval flickered and fluttered through the green. "I'll lay my wage an' share he's over a hundred. Are you so everlastin' anxious to land him alone?" Harvey's knuckles were raw and bleeding where they had been banged against the gunwale; his face was purple-blue between excitement and exertion; he dripped with sweat and was half blinded from staring at the circling sunlit ripples about the swiftly moving line. The boys were tired long ere the halibut, who took charge of them and the dory for the next twenty minutes. But the big flat fish was gaffed and hauled in at last.

"Beginner's luck," said Dan, wiping his forehead. "He's all of a hundred."

Harvey looked at the huge gray-and-mottled creature with unspeakable pride. He had seen halibut many times on marble slabs ashore, but it had never occurred to him to ask how they came inland. Now he knew; and every inch of his body ached with fatigue.

Museum Announces Important Archaeological Find

Activity Story

Below is a fictional article from a Peruvian newspaper announcing the discovery of a rare Incan artifact. In addition to the archaeological information, there are some details about the person who made the discovery. Read the article to find out all you can about the artifact and the people involved in its discovery.

LIMA, PERU. June 25, 2004—The Museum of the Nation in Lima has announced the discovery of a significant Incan artifact at an archaeological site near Puno. Found by the teenage daughter of the archaeologist supervising the site, the figurine is six inches tall and made of gold. Nadia Gallardo, aged 15, was working as an assistant to her mother, Dr. Yssela Gallardo, when she made the discovery. The statue caused considerable excitement at the site and was taken immediately to Lima for further examination.

Experts at the museum continue to study the figurine. Little information is available, except that it is solid gold, Incan, and probably dates from the early part of the fifteenth century. Scholars are divided regarding its purpose or use. Dr. Gallardo was quoted as saying that she is "very proud of her daughter's discovery" and "looks forward to the possibility of unearthing other significant artifacts at the site."

Dr. Stockmann Takes a Stand

from An Enemy of the People by Henrik Ibsen (Adapted)

Activity Story

The play takes place in a coastal town in southern Norway. Dr. Thomas Stockmann is asked to be the medical adviser to the management of a natural spa near his town called "The Baths." These Baths have made a lot of money for the town by attracting tourists. But after two years of investigation, Dr. Stockmann finds that the Baths are built on a poisonous swamp and that people who will come there for their health will become sick with fever.

Dr. Stockmann wants to warn the town about this danger, but the Mayor (his brother, Peter Stockmann) works against him, warning him that tourists will never come back to the Baths if they hear about this danger. The editors of the newspaper, Hovstad and Billing, at first say they will support him, but then turn against him. The Doctor tells the Mayor that he will call a town meeting so that the townspeople can hear the truth about the Baths. He believes that the townspeople will stand with him. Captain Horster, who alone has been willing to help Dr. Stockmann, offers to hold the town meeting in his house. The Mayor, Peter Stockmann, asks Aslaksen, a printer, to be in charge of the meeting. They try to keep Dr. Stockmann from speaking about the poisoned baths, but he speaks anyway, and accuses them all of wanting to lie about the poisoned baths because they are selfish and greedy.

Characters

DR. STOCKMANN—Medical Advisor for the Baths.

KATHERINE STOCKMANN—Dr. Stockmann's wife.

PETRA STOCKMANN—daughter of the Stockmanns; a teacher.

EJLIF & MORTEN—sons of the Stockmanns, aged 13 and 10 respectively.

PETER STOCKMANN—the Doctor's elder brother; Mayor of the Town and Chief Constable, Chairman of the Baths' Committee.

MORTEN KIIL—Mrs. Stockmann's adoptive father. His leather business has helped to poison the Baths.

HOVSTAD—editor of the newspaper, the "People's Messenger." Says that he wants things to change for the better, but does not want to "scare away" the readers of his newspaper.

BILLING—sub-editor.

CAPTAIN HORSTER—a ship's captain.

MR. VIK—the owner of Captain Horster's ship.

ASLAKSEN—a printer; president of the Householder's Association

1ST, 2ND, 3RD, AND 4TH TOWNSPERSONS/THE CROWD—Men, women, and some children of the town; the audience at the public meeting.

(The setting is a big old-fashioned room in CAPTAIN HORSTER'S *house. At the front of the room there is a platform. On this is a small table with two candles, a water bottle and glass, and a bell. The room is lit by lamps placed between the windows. The room is nearly filled with a crowd of townspeople of all sorts, a few women and schoolboys being amongst them.* DR. STOCKMANN *has been standing and speaking.)*

ASLAKSEN: We cannot allow such a serious accusation to be flung at a citizen community.

1ST TOWNSPERSON: I move that the Chairman direct the speaker to sit down.

VOICES FROM THE CROWD: *(angrily)* Hear, hear! Quite right! Make him sit down!

DR. STOCKMANN: *(losing his self-control)* Then I will go and shout the truth at every street corner! I will write it in other towns' newspapers! The whole country shall know what is going on here!

HOVSTAD: It almost seems as if Dr. Stockmann's intention were to ruin the town.

DR. STOCKMANN: Yes, my native town is so important to me that I would rather ruin it than see it do well because of a lie.

ASLAKSEN: This is really serious.

(Yelling and catcalls. KATHERINE STOCKMANN *coughs to warn her husband to be quiet, but* DR. STOCKMANN *does not listen to her any longer.)*

HOVSTAD: *(shouting above the din)* A man must be a public enemy to wish to ruin a whole community!

DR. STOCKMANN: *(with growing fervor)* What does the destruction of a community matter, if it lives on lies? It ought to be cut to the ground. I tell you—all who live by lies ought to be run out like rats! You will end by infecting the whole country; you will bring about such a state of things that the whole country will deserve to be ruined. And if that happens, I shall say from the bottom of my heart: Let the whole country be destroyed, let all these people be destroyed!

VOICES FROM THE CROWD: He is talking like an out-and-out enemy of the people!

BILLING: This is the voice of the people, by all that's holy!

THE CROWD: *(shouting)* Yes, yes! He is an enemy of the people! He hates his country! He hates his own people!

ASLAKSEN: Both as a citizen and as an individual, I am profoundly disturbed by what we have had to listen to. Dr. Stockmann has shown himself in a light I should never have dreamed of. I am unhappily obliged to agree with the opinion which I have just heard my worthy fellow citizens utter; and I say that we should show this opinion in a resolution. We will create a resolution as follows: "This meeting declares that it considers Dr. Thomas Stockmann, Medical Adviser of the Baths, to be an enemy of the people."

*(*THE CROWD *cheers and applauds. A number of people surround the* DOCTOR *and boo and hiss at him.* KATHERINE STOCKMANN *and* PETRA *get up from their seats.)*

DR. STOCKMANN: *(to the people who are hissing him)* Oh, you fools! I tell you that—

ASLAKSEN: *(ringing his bell)* We cannot hear you now, Doctor. A formal vote is about to be taken; but, out of respect for personal feelings, we shall vote by ballot. Have you any clean paper, Mr. Billing?

BILLING: I have both blue and white here.

ASLAKSEN: *(going to him)* That will do nicely; we shall get on more quickly that way. Cut it up into small strips—yes, that's it. *(To THE CROWD.)* Blue means "no"; white means "yes." I will come round myself and collect votes. *(PETER STOCKMANN leaves the hall. ASLAKSEN and one or two others go round the room with the slips of paper in their hats.)*

1ST TOWNSPERSON: *(to HOVSTAD)* I say, what has come to the doctor? What are we to think of it?

HOVSTAD: Oh, you know how headstrong he is.

2ND TOWNSPERSON: I think the doctor just goes crazy sometimes.

1ST TOWNSPERSON: I wonder if insanity runs in his family.

BILLING: I wouldn't be surprised.

3RD TOWNSPERSON: No, it is nothing more than revenge; the doctor wants to get even with somebody for something or other.

BILLING: Well certainly he wanted to get more money for his work, and he did not get it.

1ST, 2ND, AND 3RD TOWNSPERSONS: *(together)* Ah!—then it is easy to understand how it is!

MR. VIK: *(going up to CAPTAIN HORSTER, without taking any notice of the ladies)* Well, Captain, so you let enemies of the people stay in your house?

CAPTAIN HORSTER: I think I can do what I like with what I own, Mr. Vik.

MR. VIK: Then you can have no objection to my doing the same with what I own.

CAPTAIN HORSTER: What do you mean, sir?

MR. VIK: You shall hear from me in the morning. *(Turns his back on him and moves off.)*

PETRA: Was that not the owner of your ship, Captain Horster?

CAPTAIN HORSTER: Yes, Mr. Vik is my ship's owner.

ASLAKSEN: *(with the voting-papers in his hands, gets up on to the platform and rings his bell)* Ladies and gentlemen, allow me to announce the result. By the votes of every one here . . . this meeting of citizens declares Dr. Thomas Stockmann to be an enemy of the people. *(THE CROWD shouts and applauds.)* Three cheers for our ancient and honorable citizen community! *(Renewed applause from THE CROWD.)* Three cheers for our able and energetic Mayor, who has ignored any sympathy he may have for his brother! *(Cheers from THE CROWD.)* The meeting is over. *(Gets down.)*

BILLING: Three cheers for Aslaksen, the Chairman!

THE CROWD: Three cheers for Aslaksen! Hurrah!

DR. STOCKMANN: My hat and coat, Petra! Captain, have you room on your ship for passengers to the New World?

CAPTAIN HORSTER: For you and yours we will make room, Doctor.

DR. STOCKMANN: *(as PETRA helps him into his coat)* Good. Come, Katherine! Come, boys!

KATHERINE STOCKMANN: *(quietly)* Thomas, dear, let us go out by the back way.

DR. STOCKMANN: No back ways for me, Katherine. *(raising his voice)* You will hear more of this enemy of the people, before he shakes the dust off his shoes upon you . . . !

4TH TOWNSPERSON: Threatens us now, does he!

VOICES FROM THE CROWD: *(excitedly)* Let's go and break his windows! Duck him in the fjord!

A TOWNSPERSON: Blow your horn, Evensen! Pip, pip!

(Horn blowing, hisses, and wild cries from THE CROWD. DR. STOCKMANN *goes out through the hall with his family,* CAPTAIN HORSTER *pushing to make way for them.)*

THE CROWD: *(howling after them as they go)* Enemy of the People! Enemy of the People!

*(*THE CROWD *press toward the exit. The uproar continues outside; shouts of "Enemy of the People!" are heard from without.)*

The Nightingale

by Hans Christian Anderson; translated by H. P. Paull (Adapted)

Activity Story

The story I am going to tell you happened a great many years ago in China. The emperor's palace was the most beautiful in the world. In the garden could be seen the most singular flowers with pretty silver bells tied to them. Those who traveled beyond the garden's limits knew that there was a noble forest, with lofty trees, sloping down to the deep blue sea, and the great ships sailed under the shadow of its branches. In one of these trees lived a nightingale, who sang so beautifully that even the poor fishermen, who had so many other things to do, would stop and listen.

Sometimes, when they went at night to spread their nets, they would hear her sing, and say, "Oh, is not that beautiful?" But when they returned to their fishing, they forgot the bird until the next night. Then they would hear it again, and exclaim "Oh, how beautiful is the nightingale's song!"

Travelers from every country in the world came to the city of the emperor, which they admired very much; but when they heard the nightingale, they all declared it to be the best of all. And the travelers, on their return home, told what they had seen; and learned men wrote books. The books traveled all over the world, and some of them came into the hands of the emperor; and he sat in his golden chair, and, as he read, he nodded his approval every moment, for it pleased him to find such a beautiful description of his city, his palace, and his gardens. But when he came to the words, "the nightingale is the most beautiful of all," he exclaimed, "What is this? I know nothing of any nightingale. Is there such a bird in my garden?"

Then he called one of his lords-in-waiting.

"There is a very wonderful bird mentioned here, called a nightingale," said the emperor; "they say it is the best thing in my large kingdom. I would like it to come to the palace this evening." said the emperor.

"I have never heard of her," said the lord-in-waiting, "yet I will try to find her."

But where was the nightingale to be found? The nobleman went up stairs and down, through halls and passages; yet none of those whom he met had heard of the bird.

At last he met with a poor little girl in the kitchen, who said, "Oh, yes, I know the nightingale quite well; indeed, she can sing. Every evening I take home food to my poor sick mother; she lives down by the seashore, and as I come back I feel tired, and I sit down in the wood to rest, and listen to the nightingale's song. Then the tears come into my eyes, and it is just as if my mother had kissed me."

So the little girl went into the wood where the nightingale sang, and half the court followed her.

"There she is," said the girl, pointing to a little gray bird.

"Is it possible?" asked the lord-in-waiting, "I never imagined it would be a little, plain, simple thing like that. Excellent little nightingale, I have the great pleasure of inviting you to a court festival this evening."

"My song sounds best in the green wood," said the bird; but still she came willingly when she heard the emperor's wish.

The palace was elegantly decorated for the occasion. The walls and floors of porcelain glittered in the light of a thousand lamps. The whole court was present, and the little kitchen maid had received permission to stand by the door. Every eye was turned to the little gray bird when the emperor nodded to her to begin. The nightingale sang so sweetly that the tears came into the emperor's eyes,

Name ______________________________ Date ______________

and then rolled down his cheeks, as her song became still more touching and went to every one's heart. The emperor was so delighted that he declared the nightingale should have his gold slipper to wear round her neck, but she declined the honor with thanks. "I have seen tears in an emperor's eyes," she said; "that is my richest reward."

The nightingale's visit was most successful. She was now to stay at court, to have her own cage, with liberty to go out twice a day and once during the night. The whole city spoke of the wonderful bird.

One day the emperor received a large packet on which was written "The Nightingale." "Here is no doubt a new book about our celebrated bird," said the emperor. But instead of a book, it was a work of art—an artificial nightingale made to look like a living one, and covered all over with diamonds, rubies, and sapphires. As soon as the artificial bird was wound up, it could sing like the real one, and could move its tail up and down. Round its neck hung a piece of ribbon, on which was written "The Emperor of Japan's nightingale is poor compared with that of the Emperor of China's."

"This is very beautiful," exclaimed all who saw it.

"Now they must sing together," said the court, "and what a duet it will be." But they did not get on well, for the real nightingale sang in its own natural way, but the artificial bird sang only waltzes.

"That is not a fault," said the music master, "it is quite perfect to my taste," so then it had to sing alone, and was as successful as the real bird; besides which, it was so much prettier to look at. Thirty-three times did it sing the same tunes without being tired; the people would gladly have heard it again, but the emperor said the living nightingale ought to sing something. But where was she? No one had noticed her when she flew out at the open window, back to her own green woods.

"What strange conduct," said the emperor, when her flight had been discovered; and all the courtiers said she was very ungrateful.

After this the real nightingale was banished from the empire, and the artificial bird placed on a silk cushion close to the emperor's bed.

So a year passed, and the emperor, the court, and all the other Chinese knew every little turn in the artificial bird's song, and for that same reason it pleased them better.

One evening, when the artificial bird was singing its best, and the emperor lay in bed listening to it, something inside the bird sounded "whizz." Then a spring cracked. "Whir-r-r-r" went all the wheels, running round, and then the music stopped. The emperor immediately sprang out of bed, and called for his doctor; but what could he do? Then they sent for a watchmaker; and, after a great deal of talking and examination, the bird was put into something like order. Now there was great sorrow, as the bird could only be allowed to play once a year.

Five years passed, and then a real grief came upon the land. The emperor lay so ill that he was not expected to live. Already a new emperor had been chosen.

Cold and pale lay the emperor in his royal bed; the whole court thought he was dead, and everyone ran away to honor the new emperor. But the emperor was not yet dead. A window stood open, and the moon shone in upon the emperor and the artificial bird. The poor emperor, finding he could scarcely breathe with a strange weight on his chest, opened his eyes, and saw Death sitting there. He had put on the emperor's golden crown, and held in one hand his sword of state, and in the other his beautiful banner.

Suddenly there came through the open window the sound of sweet music. Outside, on the bough of a tree, sat the living nightingale. She had heard of the emperor's illness, and was therefore coming to sing to him of hope and trust. And as she sang, the shadows grew paler and paler; the blood in the emperor's veins flowed more rapidly, and gave life to his weak limbs; and even Death himself listened, and said, "Go on, little nightingale, go on."

She sung of the quiet churchyard, where the white roses grow, where the elder-tree wafts its perfume on the breeze and the fresh, sweet grass is moistened by the mourners' tears. Then Death longed to go and see his garden, and he floated out through the window in the form of a cold, white mist.

"Thank you, thank you, you heavenly little bird," said the emperor. "I know you well. I banished you from my kingdom once, and yet you have banished Death from my heart, with your sweet song. How can I reward you?"

"You have already rewarded me," said the nightingale. "I shall never forget that I drew tears from your eyes the first time I sang to you. But sleep now, and grow strong and well again."

And as she sang, the emperor fell into a sweet sleep; and how mild and refreshing that slumber was! When he awoke the sun shone brightly through the window; but not one of his servants had returned—they all believed he was dead; only the nightingale still sat beside him, and sang.

"You must always remain with me," said the emperor, "and I will break the artificial bird into a thousand pieces."

"No, do not do that," replied the nightingale. "Keep it here still. I cannot live in the palace, and build my nest. I will come, I will sing to you; but you must promise me one thing."

"Everything," said the emperor.

"I only ask one thing," she replied. "Let no one know that you have a little bird who tells you everything. It will be best to hide it." So saying, the nightingale flew away.

The Oldest of Trees

based on "The Spirit That Lived in a Tree" in *Eastern Stories and Legends*
by Marie L. Shedlock

Activity Story

Now there reigned in India a King who said to himself, "All over India, the kings live in palaces supported by many a column. I will build me a palace resting on one column only—then I shall be the best of all kings."

In the King's Park was a lordly *sal* tree, straight and well grown, and loved by village and town. Suddenly there came an order from the King that the tree should be cut down.

The people were upset, but the woodmen, who dared not disobey the orders of the King, came to the Park and spoke to the Tree. "O Tree!" they said. "On the seventh day must we cut you down, for so the King has commanded. Please do not blame us, as we are only obeying the King's command."

Hearing this, the Tree thought, "These builders are determined to cut me down. All the young *sal* trees that stand around me will be destroyed! My own destruction does not touch me so near as the destruction of my children. I must protect their lives."

At the hour of midnight the Tree went to the King's chamber and stood weeping beside the King's pillow. At the sight of him, the King was very frightened. "Who are you," he cried, "and why do you cry so?"

"In your country I am known as the Luck-Tree," the Tree said. "For sixty thousand years have I stood, and though they have built many a house, and many a town, no violence has been done to me. Please spare me, also, O King."

"Never have I seen so mighty a trunk, so thick and strong a tree," said the King, "but I will build me a palace, and you shall be the only column on which it shall rest, and you will live there for ever."

And the Tree said, "Since you must cut me down, I ask that you cut me down carefully, one branch at a time, and cut the root last."

And the King said, "O Woodland Tree! What do you ask of me? That would be a painful death. One stroke at the root would be better. Why do you wish to die slowly?"

The Tree answered, saying, "O King! My children, the young *sal* trees, all grow at my feet. If I should fall with one mighty crash, my young children of the forest would die also!"

The King was moved by the Tree's spirit of sacrifice. "O great and glorious Tree!" said the King. "Because you are willing to die for your children, I will not cut you down. Return to your home in the ancient forest."

Unit Links Reading: Ecology

King Lear

based on *King Lear* by William Shakespeare

Read-Aloud

King Lear is old and tired. He has decided to divide his kingdom between his three daughters: Goneril, Regan, and Cordelia. He brings them together, saying that he wishes to know which of them loves him best:

LEAR

Tell me, my daughters . . . which of you shall we say doth love us most,

That we our largest bounty may extend

Where nature doth with merit challenge. Goneril,

Our eldest-born, speak first.

Goneril, who does not really love her father, lies and says:

GONERIL

Sir, I love you more than word can wield the matter;

Dearer than eyesight, space, and liberty;

Beyond what can be valued, rich, or rare . . .

Beyond all manner of so much I love you.

The king, of course, likes being praised like this. He asks Regan to speak next. Regan, like Goneril, does not really love her father, but says she loves him even more than Goneril does. Again, King Lear is pleased to hear this.

Cordelia is upset by her sisters' lies. When she speaks, she refuses to flatter her father, even though she truly loves him:

LEAR

What can you say to draw a third more opulent than your sisters? Speak.

CORDELIA

Nothing, my lord.

LEAR

Nothing?

CORDELIA

Nothing.

LEAR

Nothing will come of nothing. Speak again.

CORDELIA

Unhappy that I am, I cannot heave

My heart into my mouth. I love your Majesty

According to my bond, no more nor less . . .

You have begot me, bred me, loved me. I

Return these duties back as are right fit,

Obey you, love you, and most honor you.

Lear is angry because he had hoped Cordelia would say that her love was even greater than that of her sisters. He was planning to give her the best part of the kingdom, but instead he banishes her:

LEAR

I loved her most, and thought to set my rest

On her kind nursery—hence and avoid my sight!

The Earl of Kent, one of Lear's loyal captains, tries to speak up for Cordelia, but the king is furious and shouts that he is banished as well. King Lear divides the kingdom between Goneril and Regan, keeping only one hundred knights for his own protection.

Goneril and Regan are already married, but two men have been courting Cordelia. One of them, the Duke of Burgundy, leaves when he sees she will not inherit part of the kingdom. But the King of France still wishes to marry her. Lear agrees, saying he never wants to see her face again.

Cordelia leaves and becomes the Queen of France. King Lear stays with his daughter Goneril, but Goneril is greedy. She wants everything that is the king's, even the hundred knights that he kept for himself. Her servants stop listening to the king's orders.

Meanwhile the Earl of Kent, who is still loyal to the king even though the king banished him, comes back in a disguise and becomes the king's servant. He and the Fool, the king's court jester, are the only true friends the king has.

Goneril confronts the king and tells him that his knights are making trouble in her courts, and that she does not want him to have so many knights. King Lear says these are lies and leaves to go stay with Regan instead:

LEAR

Detested kite, thou liest.

My train are men of choice and rarest parts,

That all particulars of duty know. . .

How sharper than a serpent's tooth it is

To have a thankless child. Away, away!

. . . Ha! Let it be so. I have another daughter,

Who I am sure is kind and comfortable.

Lear goes to Regan's castle, but finds her even crueler than her sister. Goneril has hurried to Regan's castle ahead of the king, and told her not to be kind to him. Regan tells King Lear that even fifty of his knights are too many to keep in her castle; Goneril says five are too many. King Lear realizes that his daughters want to get rid of him and that they do not love him. They throw him out into a wild, stormy night.

The King is half crazed with misery and anger as he wanders through the storm with the Fool. The Earl of Kent finds them and brings them to a dirty house where they can spend the night. Lear is so upset that at first he refuses, but Kent convinces him to come in from the storm.

KENT

Here is the place, my lord. Good my lord, enter.

The tyranny of the open night's too rough

For nature to endure.

LEAR

Let me alone.

KENT

Good my lord, enter here.

LEAR

Wilt break my heart?

KENT

I had rather break mine own. Good my lord, enter.

LEAR

. . . The tempest in my mind

Doth from my senses take all feeling else . . .

No, I will weep no more. In such a night

To shut me out! Pour on; I will endure.

In such a night as this! O Regan, Goneril,

Your old kind father, whose frank heart gave all—

O, that way madness lies; let me shun that.

No more of that.

The Earl of Kent takes Lear to Dover the next day, and hurries off to Cordelia to tell her what has happened.

Cordelia rushes to Dover with her army. She finds King Lear in bad shape, wandering around the fields. She takes care of him, forgiving him for everything. At last King Lear knows which of his daughters truly loves him best.

Cordelia's army fights Goneril and Regan's armies, but is beaten, and Cordelia and her father are taken captive. Goneril, jealous of Regan's share of the kingdom, poisons Regan. When the Duke of Albany, Goneril's husband, finds out the truth of all the horrible things his wife has done, he confronts Goneril. Goneril is so upset that she kills herself.

Cordelia is to be hanged in prison. The Duke of Albany tries to stop the hanging, but it is too late. King Lear comes out of the prison carrying Cordelia's body in his arms:

LEAR

Howl, howl, howl! O you are men of stones.

Had I your tongues and eyes, I'd use them so

That heaven's vault should crack. She's gone for ever . . .

KENT

O my good master.

LEAR

Prithee away.

EDGAR

'Tis noble Kent, your friend.

LEAR

A plague upon you murderers, traitors all;

I might have saved her; now she's gone for ever.

Cordelia, Cordelia, stay a little.

   Lear falls to the ground and dies, overcome with grief. The Duke of Albany asks the Earl of Kent and Edmund, the son of Regan's husband, to take over the ruling of the land. They sadly agree and leave with broken hearts.

Answer Key

	UNIT 1	UNIT 2	UNIT 3	UNIT 4	UNIT 5	UNIT 6
	Quick Quiz	Quick Quiz	Quick Quiz	Quick Quiz	Quick Quiz	Quick Quiz
1.	D	D	D	A	C	A
2.	F	H	G	G	F	J
3.	D	D	C	A	D	A
4.	G	G	H	G	H	F
5.	C	C	C	B	A	C
6.	J	F	F	J	J	H

Spanish Vocabulary List

UNIT 1

exposition exposición—el tiempo, lugar y otras condiciones del trasfondo que definen el contexto en que una historia o drama tiene lugar

Major Dramatic Question Pregunta Dramática Mayor—la pregunta principal que hace un drama

climax clímax—el punto de más suspenso de la trama

resolution resolución—el fin de un drama historia en que el problema usualmente se resuelve

UNIT 2

character personaje—una persona o animal en un drama o historia

protagonist protagonista—el personaje principal en una trama que quiere lograr alguna meta

antagonist antagonista—un personaje en una trama que pone obstáculos en el camino del protagonista

UNIT 3

abstract movement movimiento abstracto— un estilo de movimiento en que se evocan emociones e ideas a través de movimiento expresivo, no realista

rhythm ritmo—un modelo ordenado o irregular de movimientos; la velocidad y paso de un personaje individual o de la obra entera

UNIT 4

tone tono—el uso de inflexión, o tono, y volumen vocal, para comunicar un mensaje emocional

projection proyección—el uso de volumen vocal, claridad y distinción para que un público pueda oír mejor lo que dice un actor

subtext subtexto—los sentimientos interiores del personaje que no se expresan directamente a través del diálogo

UNIT 5

floor properties propiedades del piso—o "props;" objetos encontrados en el escenario

personal properties propiedades personales— o "props;" objetos usados por los actores sobre el escenario

decorative properties propiedades decorativas— o "props;" objetos no usados por los actores que establecen el marco escénico

UNIT 6

subject sujeto—una de la ideas centrales de un drama; contesta la pregunta '¿De qué se trata este drama?'

theme tema—la actitud hacia el sujeto como expresada en el drama

mood talante—el ambiente emocional de un drama

Teacher's Handbook

Table of Contents

Introduction to the Teacher's Handbook

The purpose of the Teacher's Handbook is to prepare you, as the teacher, to explore and use drama in the classroom. Theatre arts, as a component of fine arts, satisfy the human need for personal expression, celebration, and communication. As students have the opportunity to tell and retell stories, create characters, and explore production elements, they will learn more about themselves and the world in which they live.

Preparing a Lesson

Creating Journals

Before you begin using the theatre lessons in this book, have each student select a notebook to be used as a journal. A journal feature in each lesson provides students with an opportunity to draw or write in response to the lesson and to apply the lesson concepts to
real life.

Selecting Lessons

Although all 36 lessons teach important theatre concepts, some teachers may not have the time to explore all of these lessons. Eighteen core lessons have been selected and marked with an icon in the table of contents. By using the **Unit Openers,** the core lessons, and the **Theatre Technique Tips,** it is possible to meet all of the theatre standards in the National Standards for Arts Education.

Gathering Materials

▶ In the left column of each lesson is a materials list. Before class, gather any materials needed for the lesson. These often include photocopies of a lesson **Warm-Up** page. **Read Alouds** do not need to be copied, as you will read these pages aloud to the class.

▶ The last lesson in each unit is a **Unit Activity.** The stories for these lessons are in the back of the book beginning on page 124. Sometimes these stories will need to be photocopied and distributed to students; they will not need to be copied when they are a **Read Aloud.**

Using the Theatre Technique Tips

The first section in the Teacher's Handbook is the **Theatre Technique Tips.** These tips are referenced in the lessons at point of use. Each Technique Tip covers a style of Creative Expression used in the lessons, such as pantomime or script writing. Use these tips to introduce students to the techniques the first time they are used in a lesson or for review.

Exploring the Professional Development Articles

These articles provide valuable information about the use and benefits of drama in the classroom. By covering topics such as classroom management, definitions of terms, and inclusion of students with disabilities, these articles offer the support a classroom teacher needs to implement drama in the classroom.

Using the Scope and Sequence, Glossary, and Index

The **Scope and Sequence, Glossary,** and **Index** will help you find what a concept or term means and where they are covered within this and other grade levels in *Theatre Arts Connections.*

Theatre Technique Tips
Pantomime

Focus

General Definition

Pantomime is acting without words. When actors pantomime a story they use facial expressions and expressive movements to communicate. Although there are other uses of this term, in this program *pantomime* is defined as "movement that uses silent action to tell a story."

Related Concepts

► Narrative pantomime, a more specific type of pantomime, involves many actors pantomiming in unison while a story or poem is read aloud. In this type of pantomime, the actors do not interact with one another; instead, all students portray characters at the same time.

► *Pantomime* and *mime* are not synonymous. Mime is a special art form that is closely related to pantomime; however, a mime uses a specific, stylized form of pantomime to communicate an idea and theme. Mimes often paint their faces in such a way to make their facial expressions more easily seen from a distance. Miming is an intensely disciplined art, and most mimes study specialized techniques for years.

Teach

Introduce students to skills related to pantomime in one or more of the following ways:

► Relaxation allows actors to use their bodies safely and expressively. Have students relax their bodies in preparation for pantomime by closing their eyes and consciously tensing and relaxing each muscle in their bodies, beginning with their toes and working their way up to their neck muscles.

► Discuss student observations of people's nonverbal signals in real life, such as the way slumped shoulders might communicate depression or weariness. Have students imitate some nonverbal signals, working to imagine and identify each character's specific situation, thoughts, feelings, and motivation.

► Discuss the importance of interacting with invisible objects in a realistic way. Have students hold two different objects, such as a pencil and a glass, noting each object's shape and weight. Have them pantomime holding one of these objects, focusing on retaining the object's exact dimensions, weight, texture, and firmness.

► Placement is very important in pantomime. Invisible objects such as a shelf or a door handle must remain the same throughout a pantomime. For example, if an actor pantomimes setting a glass down on a table and then returns to pick it up, the glass must appear to be in the same location in space. Have students practice this by each in turn pantomiming an interaction with an object, such as opening a door, so that the object's location does not seem to change.

Reflect

Have students consider any of the following questions that apply to their exploration of pantomime:

► Did your pantomime have a distinct beginning, middle, and end?

► Describe your character's feelings and desires. How did you use your body to communicate them?

► Did you use distinct body movements?

► How could you improve next time?

Theatre Technique Tips

Improvisation

Focus

General Definition

Improvisation is spontaneous. When students work together on improvisations, they are developing skills in creativity, imagination, and listening to others. In this program *improvisation* is defined as "acting without a script or rehearsal."

Related Concepts

► Scene improvisation is situation-focused. Actors may quickly choose the characters, setting, and situation (including conflict) for a scene and then act the scene out. Although it is spontaneous an improvisation of a scene should still have a beginning, a middle, and an end through which characters solve a problem.

► Character improvisations can allow actors to further explore characters from stories or plays. They can improvise characters interacting in situations different from those in stories, such as two actors improvising a meeting between characters from different books. Actors should focus on character details and work to infer new actions and speech based on previous characterization.

Teach

Introduce students to skills related to improvisation in one or more of the following ways:

► Tell students that they should usually not "deny" by contradicting other actors during an improvisation. Say, "If another actor improvises the statement, 'I love your blue hair,' do not automatically say, 'My hair isn't blue.' Accept the believability of the situation and other actors' creativity. Use your imagination to respond."

Have the class improvise characters who wake up on a spaceship and must figure out how to get back to Earth.

► Explain that during an improvisation, actors avoid asking questions, especially questions that are answered with *yes* or *no*. These shut down the action of an improvisation. Have student pairs improvise the following: one student chooses the basic identities of two characters and their situation but keeps them secret from the other student. As they improvise the scene the student who does not know the secret facts may not ask direct questions about the facts, but must instead follow the other character's lead.

► Say, "Actors must focus on their characters' motivation and the conflict in the improvisation." Create an improvisation at a bus stop. Have each student decide on the facts of a certain character, including his or her motivation for being at the bus stop. Begin the improvisation, allowing students to go and wait at the bus stop as their characters and to interact with each other.

Reflect

Have students consider any of the following questions that apply to their exploration of improvisation:

► What were some challenges of "thinking on your feet"?

► Did you keep your focus on the facts of your situation and characterization? Did you work toward your character's goal?

► Did you accept others' ideas onstage?

Theatre Technique Tips
Theatre Games

Focus

General Definition

Theatre games are closely related to improvisation. In this program *theatre game* is defined as "an active game that helps students focus on some aspect of performance skills or story development."

Related Concepts

► Many theatre games focus on problem-solving skills by asking students to accomplish a goal, or focus, while observing certain rules. A student is successful during a theatre game when he or she keeps the focus and accomplishes the goal. A theatre game might involve organizing actions into a sequence of events, showing emotion through arm or leg movement alone, showing feeling using a made-up language, or group creation of a movement machine through use of repeated movements.

► It is often helpful to use a technique known as sidecoaching, or calling out phrases or words, to help students keep their focus on solving a problem. If students play a theatre game that is a slow-motion version of freeze tag, you might say things like, "Remember to move in slow motion! Control your bodies."

Teach

Introduce students to skills related to theatre games in one or more of the following ways:

► Remind students that being funny or clever is not the focus of theatre games. One type of theatre game involves creating an emotion machine. Choose an emotion, such as joy, and have one student begin repeating an action and a word or sound to illustrate joy, such as throwing his or her arms up and saying,

"Hooray!" Other students should add their own repetitive actions and speech or sound to the machine, but their actions must be reactions to another student's action.

► Tell students that theatre games help them focus on listening to and watching each other carefully when they work together. Another theatre game is called the mirror game. Have student pairs sit across from each other. One student should act as the leader, while the other must mirror the leader's actions. They should focus on making it impossible to tell which student is the leader.

Reflect

Have students consider either of the following questions that apply to their exploration of theatre games:

► What was the focus of the theatre game you played? Did you keep that focus?

► How do you think theatre games help actors become better at playing characters?

Theatre Technique Tips
Dramatization

Focus

General Definition

Story dramatization is an important aspect of drama in the classroom. It allows students to better understand and interpret written texts by enacting the events from stories. In this program *dramatization* is defined as "using movements and dialogue to act out a scene from a story, book, play, or other text."

Related Concepts

► Dramatization is related to improvisation in that students are not required to memorize lines; however, dramatization differs from improvisation in that the characters, situations, and storylines are predetermined and fixed.

► Some story dramatizations might not involve speech; such dramatizations would be defined as pantomimes in our program, as the focus would be on physicalizing stories. Dramatizations involving dialogue without action are not categorized separately unless students are presenting a certain type of script dramatization known as Reader's Theatre.

Teach

Introduce students to skills related to dramatization in one or more of the following ways:

► Choose a book students have recently read as a class and a specific scene. Have students identify when and where the scene takes place, the weather, actions performed by the characters, the characters' attitudes and feelings, and any other relevant information. Have groups of students assign roles and discuss how to use speech and movement to act out this scene as the characters. For younger students, you may find it helpful to read the scene aloud, pausing at certain places to allow student groups to act out what you have just read. Discuss any choices they had to make about details that were not described in the book.

► Read aloud a narrative poem, such as "A Remarkable Adventure" by Jack Prelutsky. Have students listen carefully and then write or describe the events from the poem in order. Divide students into groups that contain the appropriate number of actors. Have student groups assign roles and decide how they are going to act out the characters' actions. Reread the poem, and then have student groups share their speech and actions with the class. Discuss how dramatizing the poem changed the students' understanding of the events.

Reflect

Have students consider either of the following questions that apply to their exploration of dramatization:

► Compare and contrast your dramatization with the book or story you dramatized. Did you change anything?

► How did your dramatization help you better understand the original story?

Theatre Technique Tips
Tableau

Focus

General Definition

A tableau is often used as an acting exercise, but it may also be used to begin or end a scene in a play. In this program *tableau* is defined as "a living snapshot or sculpture formed with actors' bodies that shows a moment of action in a story or illustrates the theme of a story."

Related Concepts

► Tableau is closely related to pantomime, as in tableaux actors must use their body positions and facial expressions to communicate characters and situations. Unlike pantomime, actors cannot use movement to further communicate. In a tableau, actors may use stylized body positions and exaggerated facial expressions.

► A tableau may be based on imaginary or historical characters and situations, or may illustrate character relationships from a book, play, or other existing text.

Teach

Introduce students to skills related to tableaux in one or more of the following ways:

► If students have not created tableaux before, you may wish to begin by having them improvise a situation or dramatize a story. Tell them to freeze, and have other students examine their body positions, describing what they know about the characters and their situations through the tableau alone. Allow student groups to plan their tableaux the second time through, choosing body positions and facial expressions that might better show their feelings and relationships.

► Show students the image of an appropriate photo, painting, or sculpture, and have student groups create tableaux based on this work.

► Have older student groups create tableaux illustrating the theme of a story or the moral of a fable. For example, students might illustrate the moral, "A friend in need is a friend indeed" by creating a tableau in which one character is helping another character study for a test. Discuss different interpretations of each theme or moral.

► Tell students that when creating a tableau, especially one based on a made-up situation, they need to make concrete decisions about their characters and relationships. If students do not seem to be doing this in their tableaux, hold an imaginary microphone in front of different students within a tableau, and have them speak their characters' thoughts. Take suggestions from the class as to how the bodies of the students in a tableau could show their thoughts and feelings.

Reflect

Have students consider any of the following questions that apply to their exploration of tableau:

► How would you compare and contrast tableaux and photographs or paintings?

► How did your tableau show who each character was and what his or her relationships were to the other characters?

► What was challenging about creating your tableau?

Theatre Technique Tips
Puppetry

Focus

Puppetry involves giving life to and creating characters from objects. In this program *puppetry* is defined as "bringing an object to life in front of an audience."

Related Concepts

► Shadow puppets are figures, usually two-dimensional, which are manipulated behind a screen, or stretched cloth. When a light shines on the puppets from behind the screen, they cast shadows on the screen. Sometimes actors use their hands or bodies as shadow puppets; actors may also use their bodies to create a montage, or shadow tableau.

► Stick puppets are cut-out shapes attached to items such as craft sticks.

► Hand puppets are puppets that fit over actors' hands like gloves. Sometimes they have moveable mouths; other times they may only have movable arms and heads.

► There are many types of puppet theatres or stages. For use in the classroom, students may create a simple stage by covering a table with a large blanket, kneeling behind it, and moving their puppets as if the top of the table is the puppets' "floor." A more complex, traditional European stage involves a three-paneled or enclosed structure. The front panel of this theatre has an opening or hole and may have curtains that open and close. Puppeteers sit within the structure and use the opening as a proscenium puppet stage. This type of puppet theatre could be simulated by cutting an opening in a trifold presentation board.

Teach

Introduce students to skills related to puppetry in one or more of the following ways:

► Creating puppets may involve a few simple steps or may become very complicated. To introduce students to hand puppet creation, bring in socks or mittens and allow students to glue or sew on facial features using jiggly eyes, sequins, yarn, or beads. Tell students to make a list of their characters' traits before beginning. Appropriately tailor the complexity of the materials and methods involved to the age of the students.

► Explain that when a hand puppet talks, its entire body should move. Other puppets onstage should freeze to indicate they are "listening." When using a moveable mouth puppet the student's fingers should move the puppet's head while his or her thumb should move the mouths. The thumb only should be moved when a puppet is speaking. Puppeteers must work to match their puppets' mouth movements to their speech. Puppets appearing from below a table stage should gradually enter while bobbing up and down as if climbing a flight of stairs; when they exit, puppets should seem to go back down a flight of stairs.

► Have older students create puppets with jointed arms and legs attached to rods; show examples of similar puppets from Jim Henson's Muppets or Indonesian shadow theatre.

Reflect

Have students consider either of the following questions that apply to their exploration of puppetry:

► What can you do as a puppeteer that you cannot do as an actor and vice versa?

► How could you better match your puppet's mouth movements to the words you speak?

Theatre Technique Tips
Reader's Theatre

Focus

Reader's Theatre allows students to focus on vocal characterization and sound effects. In this program *Reader's Theatre* is defined as "a style of theatre in which performers read from a script, creating characterizations through their voices, facial expressions, and upper-body posture."

Related Concepts

► Choral readings, in which groups or individual actors speak or chant lines, were popular in speech and drama competitions of the 1930s and 1940s. They are thought by some to be the predecessor of modern Reader's Theatre.

► Reader's Theatre is a presentational style of theatre; in other words the audience never forgets that what they are watching is not real life, but rather a dramatic presentation. All physical action must be imagined, as actors usually sit or stand and face the audience. Settings and costumes are limited or nonexistent.

► Reader's Theatre provides developing readers with an excellent opportunity to practice fluid reading. Although scripts are not memorized, always allow students time to rehearse their performances so that readers at all levels will be prepared.

Teach

Introduce students to skills related to Reader's Theatre in one or more of the following ways:

► Encourage students to underline or highlight the parts they read. Pauses or breaks in reading, determined through rehearsing, should be marked in some way to aid the reader. Students should decide whether they wish to use audience focus, in which all performers look at the audience while reading, offstage focus, in which performers look above the heads of the audience as if they are speaking to other, invisible characters, or (less traditionally used) onstage focus, in which performers look at one another when reading.

► Oral interpretation practice is important. Students need to experiment with vocal pitch, range, quality, intensity, and inflection, and learn what their voices can do. One way to do this is to present students with a simple nursery rhyme, such as "The House That Jack Built." Challenge students to say the rhyme and resist speaking in a sing-song fashion. Have them focus on the verbs and find different, appropriate ways to say them. For example, how might the verb in the line "that *kissed* the maiden all forlorn" be said differently from the verb in the line "that *killed* the rat"?

► Actors in Reader's Theatre often play more than one part, and doing so presents interesting challenges in vocal characterization. Have pairs of students select, adapt, or write a script containing four or more characters to perform as Reader's Theatre; challenge them to divide the roles and find ways to use their voices and facial expressions to indicate each character. They may wish to rewrite some of the descriptions of action so that they may be read by a narrator.

Reflect

Have students consider either of the following questions that apply to their exploration of Reader's Theatre:

► Was it challenging to act through voice and facial expressions? Why or why not?

► How did the Reader's Theatre performance help you better understand the reading selection?

Theatre Technique Tips

Script Writing

Focus

Writing a play allows students to directly connect skills in language arts with skills and knowledge about theatre. In this program *script writing* is defined as, "creating improvised dialogue for a monologue, short scene, or play and formalizing that dialogue by recording it or writing it in a script format."

Related Concepts

▶ Playwriting involves mastering the steps of the writing process, including inventing characters and plot situations, writing drafts, presenting readings, revising, and publishing or producing the finished work.

▶ Unlike writers of novels or short stories, a playwright's work is not fully finished until it is performed. Playwrights often revise scripts based on problems or ideas that arise during rehearsals and production.

Teach

Introduce students to skills related to script writing in one or more of the following ways:

▶ Younger students may not be able to write their own scripts. Script writing in this case should involve creating characters, improvising and refining dialogue, and recording this dialogue using audio or video recording. After reviewing their recorded dialogue, have students discuss whether their dialogue told a story with action and a beginning, a middle, and an end. Was their dialogue appropriate? Allow students to revise and replay their scripts.

▶ Encourage students to write character sketches, story ideas, and interesting verbal phrases or overheard dialogue in notebooks or journals. These ideas can be very useful when working on a script in which they are creating new and imagined characters.

▶ Encourage students working on script ideas to decide on a through line, or major action of the play, and conflict early on. What will be their story's Major Dramatic Question? What is its five Ws? Who are the protagonist and antagonist(s)? Improvising scenes as invented characters can help students develop both character and plot ideas.

▶ Remind students that character dialogue should fit the characters. Their words and phrasing should match their personalities, times in which they live, social and economic situations, and emotional state. Students should also consider how easily their scripts can be staged.

▶ Have students use traditional script formatting. Characters should be introduced in a list form at the beginning of the script. When a character speaks in the play, his or her name should be set to the left of the line and be followed by a colon or period. Stage directions and descriptions of a character's attitude when speaking should be set in parentheses and italics (or should be written in a different color of ink if handwritten).

Reflect

Have students consider any of the following questions that apply to their exploration of script writing:

▶ Did your scene, monologue, or play have a clear beginning, middle, and end?

▶ Who was your protagonist or main character? What did he or she want to achieve? What obstacles made this goal difficult to pursue?

▶ How would you like to stage your play? Who would you cast as your characters?

Theatre Technique Tips
Storytelling

Focus

Storytelling is one of the most ancient theatrical art forms. In our program *storytelling* is defined as "the art of sharing stories with other people."

Related Concepts

▶ Throughout history, storytellers have served an important purpose. In preliterate cultures a storyteller was the keeper of a culture's history, beliefs, and traditions. Stories had to be passed from one generation to another, and thus traditional stories were often structured in a way that made them easier to remember, such as creating groups of three characters or events or repeating certain phrases over and over within a story.

▶ Storytelling in America has experienced a revival in the last hundred years. In the early twentieth century, American libraries first began to offer story hours for children. A few professional storytellers from England and Europe came and taught storytelling techniques to librarians, teachers, and many other interested people. In 1903 Richard T. Wyche organized the National Story League at the University of Tennessee, which began a revival of the art of storytelling in the South. Today there are many ways to experience American storytellers through live or recorded performances.

Teach

Introduce students to skills related to storytelling in one or more of the following ways:

▶ Storytelling is closely related to acting. A storyteller should use vocal and facial expressions to create characters and engage an audience. Give students time to practice telling stories they plan to share with others, working in groups to give each other constructive feedback to help improve each story. Storytellers should focus on making eye contact with the audience. They should focus on the audience's responses, slowing down, speeding up, and emphasizing parts of their stories so that the audience fully engages with and understands a story.

▶ Stories explaining how something in nature came to be are told throughout the world. Have students select a phenomenon or object in nature, such as the rainbow or the sun. Allow them to make up stories explaining its beginning, such as where the first rainbow came from or why the sun seems to cross the sky.

▶ Students may find it helpful to create outlines of stories they plan to tell. They do not need to memorize stories, but they should have a clear understanding of the order of events.

▶ Storytelling in the classroom can provide students with a way to share personal stories or stories from their heritages. Have students share such stories.

▶ There are many interesting storytelling traditions from other cultures, such as the "call-and-response" tradition in some parts of Africa. Have students research different storytelling traditions from cultures around the world and restructure a familiar story to match each of these styles.

Reflect

Have students consider either of the following questions that apply to their exploration of storytelling:

▶ How did you change your voice when you spoke as different characters? Were you able to keep each characterization consistent?

▶ What memory techniques could you use to help you remember the sequence of events in a story?

Theatre Technique Tips
Creative Movement

Focus

In this program *creative movement* is defined as "nonrealistic, expressive movement that allows a performer to communicate a concept or idea, such as joy or struggle, or to become a natural force or object, such as the wind."

Related Concepts

► *Creative movement* is a term constructed to cover a variety of movement styles that involve elements of dance. Rather than being realistic character movement, creative movement allows students to express themselves through improvised, free-form movement.

► Exploration of movement is an important tool for actors. It can be used as a valuable warm-up to get creative ideas flowing, and it can help actors overcome their inhibitions.

Teach

Introduce students to skills related to creative movement in one or more of the following ways:

► Choose pairs of contrasting ideas or emotions, such as freedom and bondage or terror and peace. Have students move around the room in a way that expresses one of these ideas; for example, they could stretch out their arms and then contract their bodies while looking around to show terror. When you use a signal such as a sound or word, they should change their movements to express the contrasting idea. Discuss the different types of movement that best showed each concept.

► Creative movement can be useful as a warm-up when portraying unusual fantasy characters. Have students choose a fairy tale or myth in which natural forces are personified, such as "The Rat Bride" from Japan. As a class, explore different creative movements that could show the force of the wind or the movement of waves. Work to incorporate these movements into actors' performances as these characters.

► Have students attempt to show an idea or emotion using controlled, repetitive movement of isolated body parts, such as their arms or feet alone.

► Discuss plays or performances in which abstract movement could be used. For older students, connect creative movement with presentational theatre, or theatre in which actors do not seek to emulate real life but rather are clearly presenting a performance.

Reflect

Have students consider either of the following questions that apply to their exploration of creative movement:

► How did using creative movement affect the way you felt while performing?

► What types of movements did you use? How did you use isolated body parts? How did you use rhythm and repetition?

Theatre Technique Tips
Dramatic Movement

Focus

When students use dramatic movement they practice showing characters through their posture and movement. In this program *dramatic movement* is defined as "a characterization exercise in which the focus is on revealing character through movement."

Related Concepts

▶ In the context of acting, dramatic movement can be very useful in building a character. Actors often use movement exercises, such as moving as their characters performing everyday tasks like getting dressed, to explore particular characters and to help them make choices about the way they will move onstage.

▶ Dramatic movement differs from pantomime in that it is not concerned with plot or conflict, but instead focuses wholly on physical characterization.

Teach

Introduce students to skills related to dramatic movement in one or more of the following ways:

▶ Choose a time period students have been studying in social studies. Discuss the types of dress worn by people in that time and culture, how people may have related to one another, and daily activities they probably performed. Have students use prop or costume pieces to help them understand the way people in that time would have moved; for example, they could simulate bustles by tying pillows onto themselves. Have students each select one character from this time period and act as this character getting dressed or preparing a meal.

▶ Have students all move as the same character performing a simple task, such as setting the table for supper. Call out different characters, such as a ballet dancer, a baby, or a penguin, and have students show the way each character might perform the activity.

▶ Have students choose animal characters. Assign each student a different emotion, and then have students move as their animal characters would move when affected by each emotion.

Reflect

Have students consider any of the following questions that apply to their exploration of dramatic movement:

▶ How did you hold your body when acting as your character? Compare and contrast this movement style with the way you usually move in real life.

▶ How did motivation and emotion influence the way you moved as your character?

▶ How did you keep your characterization consistent? Was it challenging to do so? Why or why not?

Theatre Technique Tips
Sound Effects

Focus

Creating and using sound effects in a theatrical performance is an important element of production. In this program *sound effects* are defined as "sounds and music created and used onstage to motivate action, communicate setting, or create mood."

Related Concepts

► Sound effects are an essential element of production. Sound effects used in live theatre may be live, or created at the time they are needed, or recorded prior to the performance. Mechanical sound effects help motivate action onstage. Environmental sound effects help create setting and mood; in radio drama these types of sound effects are vital to creating an image in the mind of the listener.

► Music in a performance can serve many of the same functions as sound effects. Music is sometimes a part of a scene's setting, as in the music played during a scene set at a ball. Transitional music plays between scenes and helps maintain the play's mood. Incidental music is another type of music used in plays; it is played in the background of a scene and also helps to create mood.

► Sound effects can be created using many common items. Crinkling cellophane paper can create the sound of a fire burning. Students can "walk" heavy boots across two layered boards or a box filled with gravel to create footsteps. Teacups and saucers can create the sound of rattling dishes. Large metal spoons clinked together sound like swords in a duel. A synthesizer can be used to create many interesting sound effects.

Teach

Introduce students to skills related to sound effects in one or more of the following ways:

► Have students watch a scene from a video and then make a list of all the sound effects. Replay the scene, and compare it with students' lists. Alternatively, have students watch a scene from a video with sound muted, and have them predict the effects used.

► Have students bring in recordings of their favorite music; select several of these and discuss the types of feelings each song evokes. Have groups of students improvise scenes that reflect each mood.

► Read aloud or discuss a story that takes place in a specific location, such as "Hansel and Gretel," which takes place in a forest, or bring in a book of age-appropriate scripts for older students to analyze. Discuss different possible sound effects, such as sounds that evoke setting (crickets chirping, city sounds) and sounds that motivate action onstage (a doorbell ringing, a car horn honking). If you wish, have groups of students create and record several of the necessary sound effects.

Reflect

Have students consider either of the following questions that apply to their exploration of sound effects:

► How does music affect your mood? How did you use music or how could you use music to create mood in a drama?

► Which sound effects were most effective? What are some of the challenges of creating and using sound effects for live theatre?

Theatre Technique Tips
Sensory Recall

Focus

Sensory recall or sense memory is a tool many actors use in the process of characterization. In this program *sensory recall* is defined as, "the use of remembered sights, sounds, smells, tastes, and textures to define character."

Related Concepts

► Sensory recall can be very useful to actors onstage. If an actor is supposed to act as though a cup of water is actually a cup of hot tea, he or she can use memories of the sensation of drinking a hot beverage to help create realistic reactions onstage.

► Characters' reactions to sensory stimuli can also communicate information about who they are or how they are feeling. When actors use sensory recall, they use their imaginations to transport themselves as their characters into particular situations, taking into account the characters' ages and physical, social, and emotional states.

► To use sensory recall, it is easiest to think about the small details of a memory. For example, instead of trying to remember how it feels to be hot by thinking about "hotness," remember how sweat feels as it trickles down the back of your neck or the sticky feeling of a sweaty shirt clinging to you. As an actor, using this memory and then physicalizing actions that one would take in response to it—for example, pulling at the clinging shirt or wiping the sweat off of your neck—will help recreate the sensation.

Teach

Introduce students to skills related to sensory recall in one or more of the following ways:

► Discuss with students the importance of imagination when acting. Pass around concrete objects, such as a coin, a brittle leaf, and a heavy book. Then have students pretend to pass around these same objects. Encourage them to use their memories of their previous interactions with these objects to help them imagine them.

► Have students choose a particular character and scene from a book they recently read as a class. Discuss physical sensations the character experiences in that scene. Have students identify experiences of similar sensations they have had, and have all students simultaneously move as that character, using those remembered sensations to help them act as the character.

► Discuss ways in which students could use details of sense memories they have when playing a character in a fantastic or unusual situation, such as a character who is experiencing life on another planet. How could they identify with that character's physical experience?

Reflect

Have students consider either of the following questions that apply to their exploration of sensory recall:

► How vivid or concrete was your memory of smells, tastes, and other physical sensations? Was it difficult to transfer the memory to the character's experience? Why or why not?

► How could you use sensory recall to help you better create a character who seems realistic?

Theatre Technique Tips
Emotional Recall

Focus

Emotional recall is another tool many actors use in the process of creating a character. In this program *emotional recall* is defined as "the technique of using emotional memories in the process of characterization."

Related Concepts

► Emotional recall is closely associated with a type of acting known as "the Method." The Method involves acting techniques advocated by Constantin Stanislavsky, one of the cofounders of the Moscow Art Theatre in 1898. Stanislavsky rejected acting methods of his day that seemed stilted and unnatural and wrote three famous books describing what he considered to be a more naturalistic approach to acting.

► Actors use emotional recall to help them enter the lives of the characters. If an actor cannot identify with a character's emotions in the given circumstances, he or she can find a memory that evokes that emotion. For example, if you cannot imagine the feeling of terror of a character in unusual danger but hate going to the dentist, you might use the memory of sitting in the waiting room of a dentist's office to identify with the character. Emotional and sensory recall are related, as specific physical details of a memory often help create that feeling. The feeling should then be applied to the characterization; actors do not think about their own memories in performances but rather make their experiences synonymous with the characters' experiences while in rehearsals.

Teach

Introduce students to skills related to emotional recall in one or more of the following ways:

► Discuss the ways students' memories of situations evoke emotions for them. How do specific details of those memories, such as sounds or smells they remember, make each memory seem more real?

► Have students close their eyes and recall a common event, such as arriving at school on the first day. Ask questions to help them remember details of that event, such as, "What was the weather like that morning? What clothes were you wearing?" and so on. After a few minutes, have students open their eyes and write journal entries describing any emotions the exercise evoked and what remembered details seemed to evoke the emotions. Explain that actors often use such details to help them experience and understand a character's feelings in a play.

► Have students choose an emotionally charged scene from a story or book. Discuss the way each character is probably feeling, using evidence from the text. Have students consider what memories from their own lives might help them empathize with each character's emotions.

Reflect

Have students consider any of the following questions that apply to their exploration of emotional recall:

► What remembered details most strongly evoked an emotion?

► Why do you think the concrete details of a memory help recreate feelings you had long ago?

► In what various character situations could you use this specific memory?

Theatre Technique Tips
Settings

Focus

Settings in live theatre are created visually through a combination of scenery, props, and lighting. In this program *setting* is defined as "the visual elements that combine to show when and where a play takes place and to evoke mood."

Related Concepts

► In professional theatre, setting is created visually through a set and lighting. Students have an opportunity to experience some of the elements of theatrical production when they create or design settings or sets for dramas. In a classroom environment, settings do not need to be very complex; the important thing is for students to consider the time and location in which a play takes place and utilize available resources to suggest that time and location. For example, students can drape blankets over chairs or desks to create scenery that evokes mountains or waves. Students might paint or draw a scenic backdrop, hang it, and then dramatize or improvise a scene in front of it.

► Although props are a part of the creation of setting, the use of props is covered separately on page T20.

Teach

Introduce students to skills related to settings in one or more of the following ways:

► Have students each make a list of every visual detail they can remember that is related to a familiar setting. Discuss their lists. What elements would be essential when communicating that location to an audience? What elements would not be necessary? Discuss choices that set designers must make when creating limited or streamlined sets.

► Sets are not always realistic. Sometimes scenery or props may be used symbolically to show a central theme of a production or to create mood. Older students may enjoy the challenge of creating set designs that show the theme or mood of a familiar book. You might also challenge them to create an abstract, symbolic setting for a play version of a favorite film.

► Discuss how details of setting affect characters in a scene. How can actors show setting through movement alone? Have students move as a character from a story with which they are familiar. Call out changes to the character's setting and have students adjust their movements. For example, if the story takes place in a desert, change the setting to a ship at sea and have students adjust their movements.

Reflect

Have students consider any of the following questions that apply to their exploration of settings:

► How did you create setting through your design, set creation, or movement?

► If you created scenery, how did it help show time, place, mood, and/or theme?

► Do you think sets are an essential element of theatre? Why or why not?

Theatre Technique Tips
Costumes

Focus

Costumes are an important part of play production. They help show who a character is and when and where a play takes place, and they are part of the overall visual design of a play. In this program *costumes* are defined as "the clothing and accessories worn by actors in a drama."

Related Concepts

► For students to fully explore the details of theatre it is important that they begin to identify and experiment with the role of clothing in characterization. In professional theatre other factors beyond characterization must be considered when costumes are designed. The costumes must both reveal characters and relate visually to the overall design and tone of a production.

► In classroom drama students should begin by experimenting with simple costume pieces, such as hats or scarves. For simplicity's sake, students can create costume pieces using materials such as paper grocery bags or posterboard. Make sure that all available materials are age-appropriate, and help younger students by performing tasks such as stapling or cutting through thick board.

► Although makeup and masks are a part of costume, their use is covered separately on page T19.

Teach

Introduce students to skills related to costumes in one or more of the following ways:

► Have students each choose one character from a book with which they are familiar. Tell them to imagine they must reveal this character through one costume piece only. What would be essential for that character? Have students each describe the costume piece and explain why it best shows who that character is.

► Have students attend a live amateur or professional theatre performance; alternatively, have them view a recording of such a performance. Discuss the ways in which costumes related to the style and color of the scenery and props. How did they help reveal who each character was?

► Have older students do further research on clothing related to a culture or time period they are learning about in their social studies curriculum. You may wish to have them do image searches using an Internet search engine as well as use printed resources such as encyclopedias and other books. Have each student use his or her research to create a costume design for a character from that time period. Discuss choices a costume designer might make that could depart from strict authenticity and why he or she might make such choices.

Reflect

Have students consider any of the following questions that apply to their exploration of costumes:

► How did the five *W*s of the story relate to your design of costumes? How did your costume reflect the character and setting?

► How did you use color in your costume?

► What types of considerations must a costume designer make when he or she is designing costumes? Why do you think he or she ought to work with the set and lighting designers?

Theatre Technique Tips
Makeup and Masks

Focus

Makeup and masks help reveal who characters are. Makeup may merely accentuate an actor's features. It can be realistic or fantastic. In this program *makeup* and *masks* are defined as "elements used to highlight or alter an actor's face."

Related Concepts

► Masks have been used in cultures around the world. Often performers have used masks for ceremonial purposes, seeking to become, embody, or personify another person or deity. Masks change a performer's face in a drastic way—for this reason, students who are reluctant to participate in dramatic activities may find mask work freeing, as masks can allow them to perform while feeling "hidden."

► Actors in professional, live theatre often design and apply their own makeup. Makeup skills are therefore essential for actors who perform in plays. Although students may learn a few of these skills, students in younger grades should feel free to experiment with makeup elements without focusing on complex, technical skills.

Teach

Introduce students to skills related to makeup and masks in one or more of the following ways:

► For the purposes of safety, do not allow students to apply makeup on each other. Make sure that each student uses his or her own brush, sponge, or cotton ball to apply his or her makeup, and that each student has access to a mirror. Emphasize the importance of safety when using makeup near eyes, noses, or mouths, and always be sure to keep the activity on-level and age appropriate.

► Allow younger students to create masks and then use face paint to transform their faces into those of animal or fantasy creatures. Compare and contrast the way masks and makeup change their faces. Which do students prefer for certain characters, and why?

► For older students who have studied principles of visual art, it may be helpful to note that realistic makeup application involves techniques that are similar to those of a portrait artist. Highlights, shading, and color value are all important in makeup application. If possible provide students with cream foundations of various shades and makeup sponges (one per student). Have students choose foundations that blend well with their skin colors and apply a thin coat of the foundations to their faces using the sponges. Explain that this acts as a blank canvas. Have them experiment with application of lighter and darker foundations to accentuate their facial features.

Reflect

Have students consider either of the following questions that apply to their exploration of makeup and masks:

► Describe the makeup or mask you created or designed. How did your mask or makeup show who the character is?

► Compare and contrast the challenges associated with the use of makeup and masks. In what situations would one be more effective than the other?

Theatre Technique Tips
Props

Focus

Properties, commonly referred to as *props*, are an essential component of a play's setting. In this program *props* are defined as "objects found or used onstage, including furniture and items used and carried by actors."

Related Concepts

▶ There are three main types of props: floor props, personal or hand props, and decorative props. Floor props are often items such as furniture, lamps, or tables. Personal props are objects carried and used by actors; they are often small objects, such as pens or money. Decorative props are props that help reveal setting, such as a portrait or painting on a wall.

▶ Like sound effects, props can serve a variety of aesthetic and functional purposes. They can help show who characters are and when and where a play takes place. They can motivate or be an integral part of a plot. They can help create mood and show a play's theme.

▶ In classroom drama props can be simple. Use objects from the classroom whenever possible or allow students to bring in objects from home. Allow students to imaginatively pretend one object is actually another; for example, a pen could be used as a microscope or as a microphone. Have students create props using art supplies such as clay, masking tape, or posterboard.

Teach

Introduce students to skills related to props in one or more of the following ways:

▶ Explain to students that stage business, which involves the use of props and parts of the set, is an essential part of acting. Actors must seem comfortable and at ease as they interact with props onstage. The correct and safe use of certain historical props, such as swords or fans, may require special training. Have volunteers act as a character writing a letter to a friend. Discuss details of such an action and how the character might interact with props such as a pen, a desk, and sheets of paper. How would the time period affect the character's actions and the props he or she would use?

▶ Explain to students that technical rehearsals are an important part of theatrical productions. They allow the technical crew to practice performing all the technical tasks related to a production, including setting (or placing) and striking (or removing) the props. When students work with props in dramatic activities, have them practice setting and striking the props in an orderly manner. If possible have some students act as the stage crew while others work as the actors. Discuss the importance of speed and consistency when placing, moving, and removing props.

Reflect

Have students consider any of the following questions that apply to their exploration of props:

▶ How do props affect the way actors move onstage? How have they affected your own performances?

▶ What was challenging about setting and striking props?

▶ How can props create both setting and mood?

Professional Development

Planning and Managing Drama Activities

by Betty Jane Wagner
Roosevelt University

Because drama can overexcite students, it is important to establish rules and signals carefully in advance. Ideally, the students and the teacher should do this together, as planning and evaluating the effectiveness of a drama afterward are crucial parts of the whole process. You will need to freeze the action from time to time to keep the drama from spinning out of control or into silliness. You can use a bell, a couple of sharp raps on a tambourine, a loud clap, or a verbal signal, such as, "Freeze." Practice responding to the signal a few times until everyone understands.

One problem that often arises in an improvisational drama is giggling. When students are shy and embarrassed, they tend to laugh instead of staying in role and playing their parts with belief and seriousness. Talk about this ahead of time. Remind the students that when they giggle and step out of role, they make it very hard for the other students to stay focused. Tell them you will stop the drama when they find it to hard to stay serious. If only one child "loses it," go over to him or her and say, "I know this is hard for you. Please take your seat until you feel you can join us without giggling." Stop the drama entirely whenever a few students do not appear to be "with it."

Take time to establish roles before the drama begins. You might start by having everyone in the class stand as if they are, for example, an elderly woman with not enough to eat. Have all the students simultaneously pantomime the posture and facial expression of that character.

Starting with pantomime is probably the easiest way to introduce dramatic activities, especially with an unruly class. You can even do this while having the students stand beside their desks. Your goal, however, should be to arrange the room—pushing aside desks or tables as needed—so that at least half of the class can work in small groups in improvising the movements of a drama.

Remember, it is not usually important that students have an audience in educational drama. The goal is to have the *experience* of role-playing, not of evoking a response in an audience. Thus, simultaneously acting out the part of each of the characters in turn while a story is being read aloud is a good way to help students focus on each of the characters before they work in small groups to assign roles and each play a different character.

Drama Terminology

by Betty Jane Wagner
Roosevelt University

The drama activities presented in this curriculum encompass both informal drama in the classroom and the more formal theatre performance for an audience. The purpose of informal drama is to enlarge and deepen vision and understanding for the *participants*. The purpose of theatre, on the other hand, is to present an enactment of human experience in order to enlighten and entertain an audience.

When a teacher conducts an informal drama, it may be termed either *creative drama, educational drama* (or *drama in education*), or, more recently, *process drama*. The goal of all of these is an educational one: to help students come to understand human interactions, empathize with other persons, and internalize alternate points of view. There is no emphasis on training actors for the stage. Brian Way describes the goal of this type of drama as leading "the inquirer to moments of direct experience, transcending mere knowledge, enriching the imagination, possibly touching the heart and soul as well as the mind" (Development Through Drama, New York: Humanities, 1972, p. 1).

Creative drama is the older term for informal classroom drama. The action in creative drama is often suggested by a story, poem, original idea, or music provided by a child or adult. Both creative drama and educational drama may include pantomime. Both are developed through improvisation and role-playing, but educational drama is less likely than creative drama to have a beginning, a middle, and an end and to begin with a warm-up and end with relaxation exercises.

In educational or process drama, as in creative drama, the action may be introduced with a story. More commonly, however, the students are asked to confront a situation lifted from history or contemporary life. When a problem or conflict is introduced from an area of the curriculum, the students are expected to respond in role, usually as persons of authority. There is less emphasis on story and character development and more emphasis on problem solving or living through a particular moment in time. Through ritual, dramatic encounters, pantomime, writing in role, reflection, and tableaux, students enter the lives of imagined characters and play out their responses to challenges and crises. Experienced educational-drama teachers often initiate the drama or move this along by assuming a role themselves; in role, they can heighten tension by challenging the participants to respond in believable ways.

Unlike creative and educational drama, whose focus is process, the focus in theatre is on *product*— a finished, polished production for an audience. Whenever students work together to prepare a drama for an audience, they are engaging in theatre. Theatre experiences build confidence and awareness of the power of theatre elements such as movement versus inaction, sound versus silence, and light versus darkness. Students who are rehearsing in preparation for a theatre performance need to be aware of the need to project their voices so all can hear, to keep their bodies facing the invisible "fourth wall," and to use gestures and actions more deliberately in order to communicate with the audience. In theatre performance the students, as actors, must accommodate for the audience and calculate the effects of their actions on that group.

Both informal drama and formal theatre have their place in the activities of the classroom. Both share the excitement and challenge of working imaginatively in role to construct contexts, events, and interactions, and both allow participants to expand their understanding of real life and the content of the curriculum.

Developmental Stages in Educational Drama

by Betty Jane Wagner
Roosevelt University

Students who are challenged or struggling readers often shine in drama activities. Often the confidence they build in drama carries over to their approach to other school tasks. Drama teachers who meet with children only for drama sessions are often surprised to find that some of the leaders in drama work are actually having difficulty in their regular academic program. Classroom teachers report that after experiencing success in drama, students improve in other areas.

It is ironic to talk about development from a more primitive to a more advanced stage of dramatic activity given the fact that drama theorists agree that preschool and primary students are the most spontaneous and uninhibited in dramatic improvisations. As they get older, students tend to lose their belief in their roles and feel self-conscious, especially if the teacher focuses too much on performance.

In R. W. Colby's 1988 groundbreaking longitudinal study of growth of dramatic intelligence, he described developmental growth as a U-shaped trajectory. His theory is that successive reorganizations of understanding account for, for example, growth from the preschool stage of *being* a character to the middle childhood stage of *playing* a character, and from that to the adolescent stage of a return to the "notion of *being* a character, but on a higher level and with the discoveries of the previous stages available" (183). In other words, both young children and teenagers can share with accomplished actors the capacity to identify with and believe that they are the characters they are performing, but in between these stages, students resort to learning from the outside rather than from the inside of the character. It is as if they perceive acting as a "game with rules," and they are trying to figure out just what the rules are. Colby characterizes this middle-childhood stage as that of *playing* a character, or pretending to be that character and glomming onto themselves whatever attributes they think their role demands. At this stage they get better at refining their register and diction for their parts, and they learn how to create gestures and actions that an audience can respond to. In the process they often lose the spontaneity that characterizes younger children.

Cognitive psychologists in their study of the spontaneous play of early childhood have found that the proportion of time spent in symbolic pretend play declines as children grow. Of all the types of play young children engage in, symbolic play decreases as games with rules increase. Jean Piaget claimed that functional (exercise or practice) play occurs during the sensorimotor stage from birth to two years. Symbolic pretend play then takes over and reaches its height between two or three and five or six years of age. By the time a child is seven or eight, games with rules that are socially transmitted become the dominant play or ludic activity, along with constructive play. Piaget's theory could account for the change in children's involvement with drama. If by seven or eight, children then treat drama as a "game with rules," they are looking for ways to learn how to *do* drama rather than simply immersing themselves *in* a role. Only later do they return to the engaged emotional identification with a character, and by then they have internalized what they have learned at the bottom part of their U-shaped trajectories.

Howard Gardner, famous for his theory of multiple intelligences, sees growth in dramatic intelligence as critical in the development of interpersonal intelligence, an art that is in much demand in our fractured and stressful society. Students who develop diverse potentials can contribute uniquely to democratic life and appreciate the differing gifts of others. No other activity teachers can foster in the classroom contributes any more to this goal than improvisational drama.

How to Respond to Classroom Drama

by Betty Jane Wagner
Roosevelt University

Do

► Ask the children to explore a story by acting it out together.

► Respond to students in role in their drama.

► Stop the drama whenever a group of students is acting silly, and ask them if they want to continue; if so, be sure the problem doesn't recur.

► After a noisy and exciting session, have the students lie on the floor as if in their beds, and reflect on how they felt and what they thought as their characters.

► Think of ways for students in role to write diary entries, letters, or news articles for the press.

► Enter the drama yourself in role as a person who heightens the tension by introducing a problem.

► After a drama is over, congratulate the whole group for staying in role and helping the drama along.

► Talk about a drama after it is over, reflecting on whether or not persons in real situations would act the way they had.

► Create dramas that bring literature or other curricular areas alive.

► Give students opportunities to depict dramatic action through drawing, dancing, or writing.

► Reflect as a class on the drama after the lesson is over and talk about what did and didn't work.

Don't

► Imply that the goal of the drama is to perform for an audience.

► Give directions to the group in your usual teacher stance.

► Ignore the behavior of a group of students who are having trouble believing their roles and are therefore giggling, rolling their eyes, or acting foolish.

► Keep a high-action drama going so long that the students stop thinking about their roles and instead get into heightening the conflict and "hamming it up."

► Separate drama from other areas of the curriculum, such as writing or reading.

► Let the drama lose focus by letting it continue without dramatic tension and therefore become boring.

► Stop the drama to congratulate a particular student, thereby creating competition rather than encouraging teamwork.

► Tell students what to do and how to do it before they act out a story, thus confusing them with too many directives.

► Set up dramas that have no relation to what students are reading in other classes.

► See dramatization as the end point of exploring a piece of literature or curricular area.

► Grade participation in a way that singles out good performers and thus sets up competition among students.

Research That Supports Educational Drama

by Betty Jane Wagner
Roosevelt University

A solid body of research shows that informal educational drama, as presented in this curriculum, is effective in improving students' oral language, reading, and writing proficiency. For a summary of the results of studies of the effects of educational drama on language arts, see Educational Drama and Language Arts: What Research Shows (cited on page T30).

Research indicates that participation in drama leads to improved listening, comprehension, understanding of sequence, and internalization of the grammar of a story. Moreover, when students role-play in a social studies, science, or math lesson, they comprehend the subject matter better. When students are just on the edge of understanding a topic, the pressure to talk in role as if they know it will help in the forging of meaning. Because students usually feel compelled to respond in a dramatic situation, they bring to bear all they know about a person in his or her imagined shoes and often connect their recent new knowledge with their previous experience, and in the process construct new perceptions. Once they have expressed their new understanding orally, they are more prepared to write about a topic. As students assume a variety of roles in educational drama, they develop a wider range of strategies for dealing with conflicts and understanding others in the real world.

When young children play dramatically, they put themselves under pressure to use language in a more flexible and mature way. They learn very early to differentiate their voice register when talking with an imagined baby, younger child, or person in authority. In teacher-led dramas, the teacher can introduce into the drama precise vocabulary that may be unfamiliar, and the students pick up the words naturally. For example, in a drama about a hospital, young children will need to use words or phrases such as *stethoscope, urine analysis, blood test,* or *CAT scan*—all of which the teacher can supply naturally in the context of the drama. They not only expand the range of their voice register and vocabulary, but they also acquire standard dialect in an effortless way. In the process they are laying down a foundation for the acquisition of literacy because both drama and reading are symbolic acts.

Because drama is a social art, students learn that unless they cooperate and support others, the game is over. Drama also prepares children for symbolic thought. In an informal drama, real objects have to be imagined and seen in the minds of all the participants in the same way—for example, the imagined table has to be in the same spot for all of the players. In other words, the role players need to be engaging in symbolic behavior if the drama is going to work. Since all of literacy is symbolic, drama is a valuable activity to facilitate reading and writing.

Thus, although students may enjoy drama very much, it is more than fun and games. By working hard at improvisation students gain insight into the social world that surrounds them and improve their comprehension at the same time.

Theatre Arts and Students with Disabilities

by Mandy Yeager
Art Educator, Ph.D. Student
The University of North Texas at Denton

Teacher Attitudes Towards Inclusion

Any discussion of the benefits of theatre arts for students with disabilities must begin with considering teacher attitudes regarding disability and inclusion. With over six percent of all school-aged children in the United States experiencing some type of disability (United States Census, 2000), the likelihood is that students with disabilities are present in every classroom. As a result, disability becomes one of the many perspectives and voices represented in classrooms. The teacher who pays heed to diverse voices and perspectives will choose instructional methods and materials that align with the abilities and experiences of all of his or her students.

Benefits of Inclusive Theatre Arts Experiences

Students with and without disabilities have much to gain from inclusive theatre arts experiences. Research studies of students with disabilities participating in theatre arts programs report a demonstrated relationship between dramatic activities and increased academic and social skills such as oral language, on-task and courteous behavior, and conflict resolution. Positive changes in student attitudes and feelings about learning and self are most pronounced for students with disabilities.

The inclusion of students with disabilities in theatre arts programs also serves to remind teachers and nondisabled students that disability is a normal experience. Numerous studies have been conducted that prove that personal interactions with persons who are disabled are the most effective way to dispel stereotypes about disability and build equitable relationships with persons who are disabled. A curriculum and a classroom that does not ignore disability, but rather honors and addresses it, is one that prepares students for social responsibility and equity.

Practical Strategies for Inclusion

Successful adaptations for students with disabilities begin with proper attitudes towards inclusion. These attitudes should be accompanied by a willingness to obtain information about students' abilities. The Internet offers a number of resources for understanding students with disabilities. Each student with an identified disability also has an Individualized Education Plan (IEP) that details information about student learning styles, strengths, needs, and goals. The Individuals with Disabilities Education Act (IDEA) guarantees all educators of students with disabilities the right to view and receive help in implementing this plan. Other useful information about students with disabilities can be gathered through collaboration with special educators and related service personnel at the school level. These individuals can give art educators useful insight regarding successful instructional strategies and modifications for students with disabilities.

Accommodations for students with disabilities should be made in the physical space of the classroom or stage, making sure that students with mobility impairments have access to class activities. Use the principles of differentiated instruction to present material in such a way that students with cognitive disabilities can readily comprehend and apply knowledge. Provide all students opportunities to think about issues of disability through thoughtful selections of scripts and classroom activities.

Conclusion

Theatre arts have a powerful role in the education of all students, especially students with disabilities. A carefully designed program will address multiple learning and social needs of students, as well as provide them with an empowering experience.

Tips for Putting on a Class Play

✔ **Choosing a Play Script** Consider the audience and the occasion. Check for royalty fees and permission requirements. Choose plays with minimal lighting and sound. Make sure the plays require a simple set.

✔ **Young Students** It can be effective to develop a play through creative drama with five- to eight-year-olds. Begin with a good story, replay it in several different ways, and then write it down to create a script.

✔ **Director's Book** Create a director's book by cutting apart a script and photocopying the pages onto larger sheets of paper so there is space to write notes and plan blocking.

✔ **Reawaken Creativity** If a scene becomes stagnant, give students a new and unusual intention or focus, such as playing the scene in slow motion or in an angry manner.

✔ **Technical Preparations** Have students use real or temporary props in rehearsals as soon as possible. Always hold a technical rehearsal so lighting and sound technicians can practice. Practice the curtain call with actors.

✔ **Work as a Team** Encourage students to help each other out; if one student forgets a line, another should cover or ad-lib; if a sound effect is missed, students should improvise to keep the scene going.

Ideas for Cross-Curricular Theatre Activities

Social Studies

▶ Divide the class into two groups. Have one group reenact a historical event while the other group acts as a film crew presenting a message biased toward a particular viewpoint of this event. Let the tensions between the two groups mount as the drama unfolds.

▶ Have small groups of students re-create the daily family life of a tribe. At some point you should enter the scene and act as a government representative who tells them they have to leave their sacred lands. Each group should decide which object they will take with them on their journey and explain why. Allow them to confront the governmental official.

Math

▶ Any story problem in the curriculum has the potential for dramatization.

▶ Role-play a situation in which making change with play money is a natural part of the drama, perhaps taking place at imagined cash registers.

▶ Role-play restaurant visits and have students calculate the tips in their heads.

▶ Whenever a drama calls for an interior space, discuss square footage. For example, have students calculate how large a hospital must be if it has 100 rooms of 9' by 10'.

Science

▶ Have one group of students discover a negative, environmental impact of a development in a community, such as a factory or housing. Unfortunately the community is dependent on this development for its economic well-being. Allow the first group to confront other students portraying town leaders with the facts they have discovered.

▶ In small groups, have one student assume the role of an important scientist, such as Jonas Salk. Allow the others to portray people who question the validity or safety of this person's work. How does the scientist present his or her case to the larger community?

Reading/Writing

▶ Have readers write a diary entry for a character from a scene they have acted out.

▶ Have students write letters in role as one character addressing another, perhaps several years after the events in the story.

▶ Have students tell or write the story of what happened long ago in a certain building in the role of stones from that building.

An Overview of the History of Theatre

Western theatre is considered to have begun with the Dionysia, a huge dramatic festival that first appeared in fifth-century B.C. Greece. The festival was held in honor of Dionysus, the Greek god of wine and nature; it contained competitions for the best dramas. The first competitions were for tragedies, which were based on Greek mythology and told of the struggles and downfalls of central heroic characters. Tragedies were written in groups of three. Each could stand on its own, but together they formed a larger unity. The great Greek tragedy writers include Aeschylus, Sophocles, and Euripides. Soon a separate competition was added for comedies, which were also rooted in ritual and mythology, but concluded with happy outcomes and featured political or literary satire. Comic playwrights include Aristophanes and Menander. Both styles included musical accompaniment, and most plays had a chorus. Greek theatres were semicircular in shape and built into hillsides so that the seats rose up from the ground-level stage area, similar to a modern arena.

Roman theatre developed from the Greeks, who they conquered in the third century B.C. Many early Roman plays were translations and adaptations of Greek plays. However, while the Greeks preferred tragedy, comedy was more popular in Rome and was of a more vulgar nature than the satiric Greek comedy. Theatres were built on level ground instead of a hill and contained a raised stage with elaborate backdrops. Eventually the chorus was eliminated and a curtain was used for the first time. Entertainment in the first century A.D. turned to gladiatorial and nautical spectacles, and by the fifth century, Christian opposition to theatre virtually eliminated all forms of drama in the declining Roman Empire.

Western theatre appeared again in the Middle Ages when the Christian church that had originally opposed drama began using liturgical plays during Mass. In the eleventh century, medieval guilds began producing plays, which remained biblical. These plays were performed outdoors. Miracle plays (dramatizations of Christian miracles), mystery plays (which included bible stories), and morality plays (in which characters were personified virtues such as Truth) were all common.

A high point of European theatre came around the sixteenth century, when Renaissance drama developed and England experienced the Elizabethan period and the rise of William Shakespeare. The increasingly professional theatres could accommodate multiple plots and stage actions. The Globe Theatre (where Shakespeare's plays were performed) was an open-air octagonal theatre, with a large elevated stage, permanent backdrop, and roofed galleries for the audience. Shakespeare wrote tragedies, comedies, romances, and historical plays, including *Hamlet, Romeo and Juliet,* and *Henry V.*

After the Elizabethan period, enclosed theatres were built and European theatre became a more elite entertainment. Female actors appeared in legitimate English theatre for the first time. Professional acting companies developed throughout Europe, and by the eighteenth century, these companies were also in America.

The nineteenth-century Romantic era produced the melodrama, an emotional, excitement-driven play featuring the courageous hero, the innocent heroine, and the evil villain. In response to Romanticism, the French "well-made play" developed, which contained a tightly structured plot with a predictable beginning, middle, and end.

In the early twentieth century, modernist playwrights abandoned past dramatic traditions. Modernist plays followed the new style of realism, in which an invisible "fourth wall" was erected between stage and audience, and theatre strove to present a "slice of life." American drama today encompasses all eras, as theatre-goers can sample everything from modern adaptations of Greek tragedies to realistic Shakespearean reenactments.

Eastern theatre began much the same as theatre had in the West, with religious rituals. According to an ancient theatre handbook, Indian drama began when the creator god Brahma brought together song, dance, and recitation to please all social classes. Indian drama was reflexive, and not bound to the western idea that a play must have a set plot with rising action, climax, and resolution. The oldest surviving plays of this kind are the highly stylized Sanskrit plays from the first century A.D., which involved stock characters whose movements and physical responses were emphasized over speech. Sanskrit declined after the tenth-century Muslim invasions, and folk dramas became the popular theatre form. During the fifteenth-century Hindu cultural revival, regional dance dramas developed, as well as historical hero plays and social satires. These all play a role in modern Indian theatre.

Chinese drama also grew from religious roots, centering around gods and ancient ancestors. Other similarities to Indian drama include stock characters and the emphasis on physical performance over literary aspects. The height of Chinese drama came in the thirteenth and fourteenth centuries with the Zaju drama, a multi-act musical play in which all conflicts are resolved and peace is restored in the final act. During the sixteenth-century Ming Dynasty, most popular theatre was looked down upon by intellectuals. The exception was Kunqu, which took place in real time to bamboo flute music and took days to perform. Modern Chinese theatre began with the eighteenth century Peking (now Beijing) Opera. As in early Chinese traditions, the Peking opera used mythological and historical subject matter and focused on music and dance performances, but it added high-speed acrobatics and duels.

Ancient and modern Japanese theatre draws inspiration from Chinese legends, but its greatest influence is native culture. Unique to Japan is Noh drama, which dates from the fourteenth century. Noh features two actors, a singing chorus, and musicians. It has little or no plot or conflict and has no ties to realism. The Kabuki theatre of the seventeenth century catered more to the growing Japanese middle class. Kabuki, which means "singing-dancing-acting," features more individual acting roles and innovative stage machinery, such as the revolving stage, which was developed in Japan years before it was seen in the west.

Early African theatre, similar to its western and Asian counterparts, took form in religious rituals that included dancing, drumming, and mask work. Communal dancing and ceremonial performances were special events that involved all tribe members. Storytelling was another dramatic form in which spoken narration and dialogue was joined by music and dancing.

In the sixteenth century, African slaves brought their traditions to America, and a unique African American dramatic style developed from the original rituals. For example, clapping and foot tapping replaced African drums and eventually evolved into early American tap dancing. Many prominent African American playwrights appeared in the twentieth century, especially during the Harlem Renaissance. Today's theatre reflects a renewed interest in early African heritage.

Further Resources

Books and Articles

Arts Education Partnership (2002). Critical links: Learning in the arts and student academic and social development. Washington, D.C.: Arts Education Partnership.

Booth, D. H. (1987). Drama worlds: The role of drama in language growth. Toronto: Language Study Centre, Toronto Board of Education.

Booth, D. H. (1994). Story drama. Markham: Pembroke Publishers.

Byron, K. (1986). Drama in the English classroom. New York: Methuen.

Bailey, S. D. (1993). Wings to fly: Bringing theatre arts to students with special needs. Woodbine House.

Erion, P. & Lewis, J. C. (1996). Drama in the classroom: Creative activities for teachers, parents, and friends. Lost Coast Press.

Gardner, H. (1985). Towards a theory of dramatic intelligence. In J. Kase-Polisini (Ed.), Creative drama in a developmental context. New York: University Press of America.

Heathcote, D., & Bolton, G. (1995). Drama for learning: Dorothy Heathcote's mantle of the expert approach to education. Portsmouth, NH: Heinemann.

McCaslin, Nellie. (1999). Creative drama in the classroom. Pearson, Allyn, & Bacon.

Miller, C. S. & Saxton, J. (2004) Into the story: Language and action through drama. Portsmouth, NH: Heinemann.

Moffett, James & Wagner, Betty Jane. (1992). Student-centered language arts, K-12. Portsmouth, NJ: Boynton/Cook, Heinemann.

O'Neill, C. & Lambert, Alan. (1990). Drama structures: Practical handbook for teachers. Stanley Thornes Pub. Ltd.

Shah, A., & Joshi, U. (1992). Puppetry and folk dramas for non-formal education. Sterling Pub. Private Ltd.

Stewig, J. W. (1983). Informal drama in the elementary language arts program. New York: Teachers College Press.

Wagner, B. J. (1998). Educational drama and language arts: What research shows, third book in the Dimensions of Drama series. Portsmouth, NH: Heinemann.

Wagner, B. J. (1983). The expanding circle of informal classroom drama. In B. A. Busching & J. I. Schwartz (Eds.), Integrating the language arts in the elementary school (pp. 155–163). Urbana, IL: National Council of Teachers of English.

Wagner, B. J. (1990). Dramatic improvisation in the classroom. In S. Hynds & D. L. Rubin (Eds.), Perspectives on talk and learning (pp. 195–211). Urbana, IL: National Council of Teachers of English.

Wagner, B. J. (1999). Dorothy Heathcote: Drama as a learning medium, 2nd ed. Portland, ME: Calendar Islands Publishers.

Wilhelm, J. D., & Edmiston, B. (1998). Imagining to learn: Inquiry, ethics, and integration through drama. Portsmouth, NH: Heinemann.

Wolf, S., Edmiston, B. W., & Enciso, P. (1996). Drama worlds: Places of the heart, voice and hand in dramatic interpretation. In J. Flood, D. Lapp, & S. B. Heath (Eds.), Handbook of research on teaching literacy through the communicative and visual arts (pp. 492–505). New York: Simon and Schuster, Macmillan.

Web sites

American Alliance for Theatre and Education: **www.aate.com.** Offers opportunities for educators to get advocacy information and collaborate with other educators

Drama Education: A Global Perspective—Learning in, with and through Drama: **members.iinet.net.au/~kimbo2.** Contains lists of drama education resources, including downloadable lesson plans and class activities, compiled by a theatre educator

VSA arts: **www.vsarts.org.** Offers a number of free resources for arts educators

National Dissemination Center for Children with Disabilities (NICHCY): **www.nichcy.org/index.html.** Offers information on special education law (IDEA), agencies and resources for educators and parents (both national and state) and specific disabilities.

Scope and Sequence of Theatre Concepts

Plot	K	1	2	3	4	5	6
A Plot Is Events in a Story	U1OP, 1.1, 1.6	U1OP, 1.1, 1.6	U1OP, 1.1, 1.6	U1OP, 1.6	U1OP, 1.6	U1OP, 1.6	U1OP, 1.6
Plot and Sequence	U1OP, 1.1, 1.2, 1.3, 1.4, 1.6	U1OP, 1.1, 1.2, 1.3, 1.4, 1.6	U1OP, 1.1, 1.2, 1.4, 1.6,	U1OP, 1.1, 1.3, 1.5, 1.6	U1OP, 1.1 1.6	U1OP, 1.1	U1OP, 1.1
Beginning/Exposition	U1OP, 1.2,	U1OP, 1.2, 1.6		U1OP, 1.3, 1.6	U1OP, 1.1	1.1	1.2
Presents a Problem	U1OP, 1.3,	U1OP, 1.3,	U1OP, 1.3,	U1OP, 1.4, 1.6	U1OP, 1.3, 1.6	U1OP, 1.3, 1.6	U1OP, 1.3, 1.6
Presents a Major Dramatic Question						U1OP, 1.3, 1.6	U1OP, 1.3, 1.6
Complications			U1OP, 1.3	U1OP, 1.4, 1.6	U1OP, 1.4, 1.6	U1OP, 1.4, 1.6	U1OP, 1.4, 1.6
High Point/Climax				U1OP, 1.5, 1.6	U1OP, 1.5, 1.6	1.5, 1.6	1.5, 1.6
Problem's End/Resolution	U1OP, 1.4	U1OP, 1.3, 1.4, 1.6	U1OP, 1.4	1.5, 1.6	U1OP, 1.5, 1.6	1.5, 1.6	1.5, 1.6
Asking "What If?"	U1OP, 1.5	U1OP, 1.5	U1OP, 1.5	1.6	1.6	1.2	1.6
Plot and the Five *W*s				1.2, 1.6	1.2, 1.6	1.2, 1.6	

Character	K	1	2	3	4	5	6
What Constitutes a Character	U2OP, 2.1, 2.2, 2.3, 2.6	U2OP, 2.1, 2.2, 2.3, 2.6	U2OP, 2.1, 2.6	U2OP	U2OP	U2OP	U2OP
Character and the Five *W*s	U2OP			U2OP			
Actions and Feelings	U2OP, 2.4, 2.5, 2.6	U2OP, 2.4	U2OP, 2.2, 2.3	U2OP, 2.1, 2.4, 2.6	U2OP, 2.1, 2.3, 2.4, 2.6	2.3, 2.4, 2.6	U2OP, 2.1, 2.2
Motivations			U2OP, 2.4, 2.6	U2OP, 2.1, 2.6	U2OP, 2.3, 2.6	2.1, 2.6	2.1, 2.2, 2.6
Actions Produce Reactions		U2OP, 2.5, 2.6	U2OP, 2.5, 2.6	2.3, 2.6	2.3, 2.4, 2.6	2.1, 2.3, 2.6	2.1, 2.6
Characters Interrelate				2.2, 2.6	2.2, 2.6	2.4, 2.6	2.1, 2.2, 2.6
Protagonist and Antagonist						U2OP, 2.2, 2.6	U2OP, 2.2, 2.6
Characters Solve a Problem				U2OP, 2.5, 2.6	2.5, 2.6	2.5, 2.6	2.5, 2.6
Internal Characterization							2.3, 2.6
External Characterization							2.4, 2.6

Sound and Voice	K	1	2	3	4	5	6
Sound Can Tell a Story	U3OP, 3.1, 3.6	U3OP, 3.1, 3.6					
Sound Shows Setting	U3OP, 3.2, 3.4, 3.6	U3OP, 3.2, 3.4, 3.6	U3OP, 3.1, 3.6	U4OP, 4.1, 4.4, 4.6	U4OP, 4.2, 4.6	U4OP, 4.1, 4.4	U4OP, 4.3, 4.6
Sound Evokes Feelings			U3OP, 3.4	4.1, 4.6	U4OP, 4.4	U4OP, 4.1	U4OP, 4.1, 4.6
Music Evokes Feelings			U3OP, 3.2	U4OP, 4.2, 4.6	U4OP, 4.4	U4OP, 4.2	U4OP, 4.2
Voice Shows Emotion	U3OP, 3.3, 3.5, 3.6	U3OP, 3.3, 3.6	U3OP, 3.5, 3.6	U4OP, 4.5, 4.6	U4OP, 4.5, 4.6	4.5, 4.6	U4OP, 4.5, 4.6
Voice Shows Character	U3OP, 3.5, 3.6	U3OP, 3.5, 3.6	U3OP, 3.3, 3.6	4.3, 4.6	4.3, 4.6	4.3, 4.6	4.4, 4.6
Sound and Silence Communicate							4.1
Sound / Voice and the Five Ws				4.1	4.1	4.1, 4.3	
Visual Elements	K	1	2	3	4	5	6
Physically Showing Setting	U4OP, 4.1, 4.2, 4.6	U4OP, 4.1, 4.5, 4.6	5.1	3.1	5.3	5.1	5.1
Physically Showing Invisible Objects	U4OP, 4.3	U4OP, 4.2	5.5	3.1			
Creating Costumes	U4OP, 4.4, 4.6	U4OP, 4.3	U5OP, 5.2, 5.6	U3OP, 3.3, 3.6	5.4, 5.6	5.3, 5.6	5.2, 5.6
Creating Masks / Makeup		U4OP, 4.4, 4.6	5.6	3.4, 3.6	5.5, 5.6	5.4, 5.6	5.3, 5.6
Creating Setting	U4OP, 4.5, 4.6	U4OP, 4.5, 4.6	U5OP, 5.4, 5.6	U3OP, 3.5, 3.6	5.1, 5.3, 5.6	5.2, 5.6	5.4, 5.6
Creating Puppets			U5OP, 5.3	1.6, 5.3			
Choosing Props	U4OP, 4.6	4.6		3.2	5.2, 5.6	5.5, 5.6	5.5, 5.6
Visual Elements and the Five Ws				3.1, 3.6	5.3, 5.6	5.1, 5.6	

Movement	K	1	2	3	4	5	6
Realistic Movement	U5OP, 5.1, 5.6	U5OP, 5.2, 5.6	4.4, 4.6	U5OP, 5.1, 5.5, 5.6	U3OP, 3.2, 3.5, 3.6	U3OP, 3.2, 3.5, 3.6	U3OP, 3.1, 3.3, 3.5, 3.6
Abstract Movement						U3OP, 3.3	U3OP, 3.3
Rhythm	U5OP, 5.3, 5.6	U5OP, 5.1, 5.3, 5.6	U4OP, 4.1, 4.6	U5OP, 5.4, 5.6	3.4, 3.6	U3OP, 3.4	U3OP, 3.5, 3.6
Repetition	5.3		U4OP, 4.3	U5OP, 5.4, 5.6	3.4, 3.6	U3OP, 3.4	3.5
Shape and Form				5.3	3.3	3.1	3.1
Action and Inaction	U5OP, 5.5	5.4		5.2	3.1, 3.6	3.5	3.4
Action and Reaction		U5OP, 5.3	U4OP, 4.2	5.5, 5.6	3.5, 3.6	3.5	3.4, 3.6
Movement Communicates	U5OP, 5.1, 5.2, 5.4, 5.6	5.2, 5.5	U4OP, 4.4, 4.5, 4.6	U5OP, 5.1, 5.6	U3OP, 3.2, 3.6	3.2, 3.6	U3OP, 3.2, 3.6
Movement and the Five Ws				5.1	3.2	3.2	

Subject, Theme, and Mood	K	1	2	3	4	5	6
Creating Stories	6.1						
Analyzing Stories	U6OP, 6.2, 6.6	U6OP, 6.1, 6.6	U6OP, 6.1	U6OP, 6.1, 6.5, 6.6	U6OP, 6.2, 6.6	6.2, 6.3, 6.6	6.2, 6.5, 6.6
Discovering Subject	U6OP, 6.3, 6.6	U6OP, 6.2, 6.6	U6OP, 6.2, 6.6	6.1, 6.6	6.1, 6.6	U6OP, 6.1, 6.6	6.1, 6.6
Discovering Theme				6.3, 6.4, 6.5, 6.6	6.1, 6.2, 6.6	U6OP, 6.1, 6.2, 6.6	6.1, 6.5, 6.6
Discovering Mood	U6OP, 6.4, 6.5, 6.6	U6OP, 6.3	U6OP, 6.3, 6.6	6.2, 6.6	6.5, 6.6	U6OP, 6.3, 6.4, 6.6	6.2, 6.6
Showing Theme				6.3, 6.4, 6.6	6.4, 6.5, 6.6	6.5, 6.6	6.5, 6.6
Showing Mood	6.4, 6.5, 6.6	6.3, 6.4, 6.5, 6.6	6.4, 6.5, 6.6	6.2, 6.6	6.3, 6.4, 6.5	6.4, 6.5, 6.6	6.3, 6.4, 6.6
Subject and Five Ws	U6OP			6.1	6.1	6.1	
Theme and the Five Ws				6.2	6.1	6.1	

Scope and Sequence of Theatre Activities

Creative Expression Activity Type	K	1	2	3	4	5	6
Theatre Game	1.1, 1.4, 2.1, 2.5, 3.1, 3.5 6.2	1.1, 2.5, 3.3, 4.1, 5.3	1.1, 2.2, 3.5, 4.2, 5.1	1.4, 2.3, 5.2	1.1, 4.2, 6.1	6.1	1.1
Improvisation	1.3, 2.2, 2.3, 3.3, 4.1, 5.1, 6.5	1.3, 2.1, 2.6, 3.1, 3.5, 4.2, 4.6, 6.1, 6.6	1.3, 1.4, 2.1, 3.3, 4.3, 5.5, 6.2	1.2, 2.5, 4.3, 4.5, 5.5	1.2, 2.3, 2.4, 4.5, 6.5	1.2, 1.4, 2.2, 2.4, 3.4, 4.3, 4.5, 6.5	1.2, 2.2, 2.5, 3.4, 4.5, 4.6, 6.1, 6.5
Pantomime	2.4, 4.3, 5.2	1.2, 5.2	1.2, 2.5	1.3, 5.1, 5.6, 6.4	3.5, 3.6	1.3, 3.5, 3.6, 5.1	1.3, 2.4, 3.2, 3.6, 5.1, 6.3
Tableau	4.2, 5.5, 6.4	2.4, 5.4	2.4	2.2, 5.6	1.5, 2.2 3.1		6.4
Puppets			2.6, 5.3	1.6			
Shadow Puppets				5.3			
Play Writing/Recording Dialogue	6.6	6.6	6.6	2.6, 6.6	2.6, 6.6	2.6, 6.6	2.6, 6.6
Storytelling	1.2, 1.6, 3.6, 6.1	1.4, 1.5,	1.5, 1.6, 6.3	1.1, 2.4,	1.3, 4.3,	1.1	1.4, 4.4
Reader's Theatre				1.5		4.4, 4.6	1.5
Creative Movement	1.5, 5.3, 5.6, 6.3	5.1, 5.6, 6.4	3.2, 4.1, 4.6, 6.5	3.1, 4.2, 5.4,	3.3, 3.4	3.1, 3.3, 6.4	3.3, 4.2, 6.2
Dramatic Movement	2.6, 5.4	2.2, 5.5, 6.3	2.3, 4.4, 4.5	2.1, 6.2	2.1, 3.2	2.5, 3.2, 4.2, 6.3	3.1, 3.5
Sensory/Emotional Recall						2.1, 2.3, 2.6	2.1, 2.3, 2.6
Creation of Sound Effects	3.2, 3.4, 3.6	3.2, 3.4, 3.6, 6.5	3.1, 3.4, 3.6	4.1, 4.4, 4.6	4.1, 4.4, 4.6	4.1, 4.4, 4.6	4.1, 4.3, 4.6
Creation of Setting	4.5, 4.6	4.6	5.4	3.5, 3.6, 6.5	5.1, 5.3, 5.6, 6.3	5.2, 5.6	5.4, 5.6
Creation/Selection of Costumes	4.4	4.3	5.2	3.3, 3.6	5.4, 5.6	5.3, 5.6	5.2, 5.6
Creation/Selection of Props				3.2, 3.6	5.2, 5.6	5.5, 5.6	5.5, 5.6
Creation of Makeup Designs				3.4	5.5, 5.6	5.4, 5.6	5.3, 5.6
Creation of Masks		4.4	5.6				
Script/Story Dramatization		1.6, 2.3, 3.6, 6.2	2.6, 3.6, 4.6, 5.6, 6.1, 6.4	1.6, 2.6, 3.6, 4.6, 5.6, 6.1, 6.3, 6.6	1.4, 1.6, 2.5, 2.6, 3.6, 4.6 5.6, 6.4	1.5, 1.6, 2.6, 4.6, 5.6, 6.2	1.4, 1.6, 2.6, 3.6, 5.6, 6.6
Direction of Others			6.4	6.3	6.4	6.5	6.5

Glossary

A

acting portraying a character to tell a story

action everything characters do in a play

action/reaction the interplay between characters in which the action of the plot is moved forward

actor a person who portrays a character in a play

antagonist a character opposing the protagonist, or leading character

arena stage a stage surrounded by audience seating

artistic license the idea that an author or performing artist has a right to change a story's details to fit his or her conception of the story's theme and to make it work better as a plot

audience a group of people assembled to see a performance

B

blocking traveling movement onstage planned and created by directors, actors, and stage managers

C

character a person in a story, play, or poem; can be a personified animal or object

choreographer a person who plans dance movements in dance, opera, and certain theatre productions

chorus a group of actors who narrate the action of a play

climax the point in a plot where the interest, tension, and excitement are highest

comedy a humorous genre of theatre developed by ancient Greeks

complication a new event or character in the story that makes a problem more difficult to solve

conflict the problem or struggle in a story

costume the clothing, accessories, and makeup or mask worn by an actor in a play

costume designer a person who creates costumes for the actors to wear in a play

D

decorative prop an object, such as a framed portrait, used to reveal a play's setting but not used by an actor

dialogue speech between characters in a play

director the person who unifies all the elements of a play to create an artistic production

dramaturge a consultant, often employed by a theatre, who is familiar with a play, its history, other productions of a play, the playwright's other works and so on; assists in research and evaluation

E

emotional recall the technique of using emotional memories in the process of characterization

enunciation clear and distinct pronunciation

environmental sound effects sounds that convey setting and environment

exposition information in a play or story, usually revealed near the beginning, that sets up the plot's action

external complication a physical event that occurs in a play that makes a problem more difficult to solve

F

five Ws five questions that a plot can answer: *who, what, when, where, why*

five Ws and an H six questions that a plot can answer: *who, what, when, where, why, how*

floor properties objects, such as a sofa, table, or lamp, found onstage

full back stance an actor's position onstage when his or her back is to the audience

full front stance an actor's position onstage when he or she faces the audience

I

inaction a purposeful pause in onstage action

incidental music background music used to create various moods

inflection a change in pitch and volume of a voice

integral music music that is written into a script to help motivate action, sometimes played by an actor onstage

internal complication a feeling or attitude within a character that makes a problem more difficult to solve

L

lighting the use of colored gel sheets to create realistic lighting or mood lighting onstage to reveal the *when* and *where* of a play

lighting designer a person who designs the lighting for a play, both for basic illumination and for effect

lighting director the person who is in charge of running lighting

live sounds sounds created during a performance that are not prerecorded

M

Major Dramatic Question the main question presented in drama; the action of the play serves to address and answer this question

makeup cosmetic elements used to highlight or alter an actor's face

makeup artist a person who uses makeup to change an actor's appearance

mask a costume piece that covers the face

mechanical sound effects sounds used to motivate action, such as a ringing doorbell

mime an actor who uses body movements and facial expressions to portray a character or situation

minimalism a theatrical movement in which setting, gesture, and dialogue are stripped down to essentials

monologue a speech, often lengthy, spoken by one character

mood the emotional feelings experienced by the audience and created by a performance

motivation a character's reason for speech or action

O

objective the goal a character works toward in a scene; part of a character's major goal in a play

onstage on the visible stage

P

personal prop an object held and used by a character

physicality a focus on physical movement that suggests age, emotion, or physical condition

playwright a person who writes the action, dialogue, and directions for movement in a play

plot a sequence of events that forms a story or drama

presentational theatre an approach to theatre in which it is obvious that the play is not like real life

producer a person responsible for a play, movie, or show; he or she obtains the script, raises money, and finds the theatre for the production

profile stance an actor's position onstage when he or she is turned sideways from the audience

projection speaking with enough vocal force to allow an audience to clearly hear what is said

properties also called *props;* objects found onstage

proscenium stage a stage framed by an arch, forming a box with three sides

protagonist the leading character in a play

puppet an object brought to life for an audience

Q

quarter stance an actor's position onstage when he or she is turned a quarter left or right away from facing the audience

R

recorded sound a sound effect that is recorded and played during a performance

repetition in theatrical movement, a pattern of repeated movement

representational characterization an acting technique in which actors represent characters' thoughts and feelings through movement and costumes

representational theatre an approach to theatre in which the audience "suspends disbelief" and views the performance as real life

resolution the part of the plot, usually near the end, in which the plot's problems are solved

rhythm in theatre, an orderly or irregular pattern of movements; also the pace of a character or play

rising action the part of a play, usually at the beginning, in which a main problem is introduced

role the part or character that an actor performs

S

satire an ironic, farcical genre of theatre developed by ancient Greeks

scenario the outline of action in a play

scenery painted boards, screens, or three-dimensional units that form the background of a play and enclose the acting area

scenic designer a person who develops the environment for the action of the play

script a copy of a play that provides stage directions and dialogue

sensory recall the use of remembered sights, sounds, tastes, and textures when portraying a character

set the scenery, props, and furniture onstage; also a term for placing props or scenery

set designer a person who creates scenery for many types of productions

sound designer a person who decides how and when sound effects will be used in a theatrical performance

sound effects sounds and music used onstage

sound technician a person skilled at using sound equipment to create the special sound effects needed in a play or performance

spike to mark the location of large props with small pieces of tape onstage

stage crew backstage workers, including stagehands

or grips, who handle scenery, and the prop crew, who handle properties

stage manager a person who helps the director and actors by writing down blocking, scheduling, and overseeing the technical aspects of a production

stock character a character whose feelings and actions come from cultural stereotypes, for example, a crazy scientist or a damsel in distress

storyteller a person who remembers the order of events in a story and tells it to listeners in a narrative style

strike to remove props quickly from a set

subject what a play is about, usually an abstract concept such as truth

subtext the character's inner feelings and intentions not expressed directly

synopsis a brief, general review or summary

T

technical production includes stage management, lighting, sound, stage mechanics, promotions, set design, and directing

theatre-in-the-round a type of theatre in which an audience can sit around all four sides of the stage

theme the message a play or drama communicates about its subject, such as "greed will lead to trouble"

thrust stage a low, platform stage that projects into the audience

tone the use of inflection to communicate feelings

tragedy a type of drama, created by ancient Greeks, in which a protagonist comes into conflict with a greater force or person and ends with a sad, disastrous conclusion

U

universal character a character type who appears in stories and literature throughout the world

V

visual elements the aspects of a dramatic performance that the audience sees, including costumes, props, scenery, lighting, makeup, and puppets

Program Index

Items referenced are coded by Grade Level and page number.

Notes

Notes

Notes

Notes

Notes

Notes

Notes

Notes

Notes

Notes

Notes

Notes